Moving towards Internationalisation of the Curriculum for Global Citizenship in Higher Education

Valerie Clifford and
Catherine Montgomery

Oxford Centre for Staff and Learning Development

Published by
The Oxford Centre for Staff and Learning Development
Oxford Brookes University
Wheatley Campus
Wheatley
Oxford
OX33 1HX

Moving towards Internationalisation of the Curriculum
for Global Citizenship in Higher Education
Valerie Clifford and Catherine Montgomery

ISBN   978-1-873576-81-6
Published September 2011

Contents

Contributors

Michelle Barker

Michelle Barker is a Professor in the Department of International Business and Asian Studies and Senior Teaching Fellow in the Griffith Institute for Higher Education. Prior to joining Griffith in 1993, Michelle had 17 years experience in the public sector. She was Deputy Director of AIDAB Queensland (Department of Foreign Affairs and Trade), and a Social Worker in the Department of Immigration and Ethnic Affairs where she was responsible for the design and delivery of orientation and skills training to refugees and migrants. Michelle has achieved a national and international reputation as a researcher in the areas of cross-cultural adjustment, prevention of workplace bullying, and sustainability in business education. Michelle won the 2005 Individual Teacher Award in the category of Law, Economics, Business and related studies in the Australian Awards for University Teaching. She also led the team that won the 2003 AAUT Award for the application of the EXCELL Intercultural Skills Training Program at Griffith University (a programme co-developed with Prof. Anita Mak from the University of Canberra). Currently, Michelle is leading an internationalisation of the curriculum project across Griffith University as well as an Australian Learning and Teaching Council project on Internationalisation at Home.

Viv Caruana

Viv Caruana is Reader in Internationalisation and Co-director of the Centre for Academic Practice and Research in Internationalisation (CAPRI) hosted by Leeds Metropolitan University, UK. Viv has published widely in the field of internationalisation of higher education, drawing on a disciplinary background in Modern Economic and Social History and, more recently, five years experience in education/academic development at the University of Salford. Her research explores both internationalisation policy and practice and the nature of the internationalised curriculum in the context of the global knowledge economy and learning society. In collaboration with Nicola Spurling, she co-authored the review commissioned by the Higher Education Academy (2007) The Internationalisation of UK Higher Education: a review of selected material. This original work has subsequently been updated by more recently commissioned research. Other recent work explores areas such as the connections between Internationalisation and Equality and Diversity and conceptualisations of global citizenship in higher education.

Mumba Chakulya

Mumba Chakulya is a third year LLB Law student at Northumbria University and a national student ambassador for the human rights charity World Vision. Mumba is the founder of the World Vision organisation at Northumbria University. She has organised a wide range of fundraising events and is also involved in civil and political activities.

Valerie Clifford

Valerie Clifford is Deputy Head of the Oxford Centre for Staff and Learning Development at Oxford Brookes University and Director of the Centre for International Curriculum Inquiry and Networking (CICIN). She has also held leadership roles in academic development at Monash University Australia and the University of the South Pacific, Fiji. She has taught in New Zealand, Malaysia, South Africa and Belize. Valerie has worked at the policy and practice level to develop internationalised curricula for all students. She has published widely on curriculum and pedagogy from a feminist and a cultural perspective. Her current research and teaching interests are in the areas of internationalisation of the curriculum, research supervision, and academic writing.

Sally Davis

Sally Davis is a Programme Leader in the School of Health and Social Care at Oxford Brookes University, UK. She is responsible for a number of programmes in the School including Rehabilitation, Public Health, and Infection Prevention and Control. Sally is a rehabilitation nurse and worked as a senior nurse for many years in a neurological rehabilitation centre in Oxford. Sally developed and now teaches on the interdisciplinary MSc in Rehabilitation. She takes a lead in the School for supporting international students and was awarded a teaching fellowship in 2006 to take this work forward. Sally is in the process of undertaking her PhD which focuses on the cultural sensitivity of rehabilitation. This has included the collection of data in India, for which Sally was awarded a Florence Nightingale Travel Award.

Brona Farrelly

Brona Farrelly is currently undertaking a PhD in the School of Political Science and International Studies at the University of Queensland. Her research project examines the impact of childbirth on the career progression of general staff in the university sector in Australia. She has a background in social science, having completed an Honours Degree in Sociology and Social Policy at Trinity College, Dublin, before going on to complete a Masters in Equality Studies at University College Dublin.

Wendy Green

Wendy Green is a lecturer in higher education at The University of Queensland, Australia. She teaches a range of higher education courses to academic staff, with a focus on internationalisation and inclusive pedagogy. She is a member of the University's Internationalisation Policy and Strategy Committee, and the Senate sub-committee for culturally and linguistically diverse and indigenous Australians. She facilitates a community of practice, which fosters research and practice regarding pedagogy for globally responsible citizenship, and she co-facilitates the Narrative Research Network, Queensland. Her own research concerns cross-cultural teaching and learning, in relation to curriculum, staff development and student mobility.

Martin Haigh

Martin Haigh is Professor of Geography at Oxford Brookes University where he specialises in Sustainability and Geographical Education. He is a Senior Fellow of the Higher Education Academy. In 2010, he was awarded both a National Teaching Fellowship and the Royal Geographical Society's 10th "Taylor and Francis Award for Excellence in Teaching and Learning" for his advocacy of 'Global Citizenship' research on Internationalisation of the Curriculum and leadership of the high-ranked, ISI-listed, Journal of Geography in Higher Education. As a member of the Steering Executive of the Centre for Internationalisation of the Curriculum and Networking (CICIN) he works on the international development of University 'Graduate Attributes', and with a HEFCE funded team on Leadership in 'Education for Sustainability'. Recently, Martin's voluntary work with the Lotus Trust NGO on community education for sustainability within the UK's Hindu community was identified by a UNESCO team as an 'outstanding' and 'unique' example of cross-cultural education. Previously, Martin was a leader of the World Soil Conservation movement, a former (Vice) President of the World Association of Soil and Water Conservation, and co-founder of the International Association for Headwater Control. He also leads international land reclamation and hazard mitigation research teams in Wales and the Kumaun Himalaya.

Ray Hibbins

Ray Hibbins is a sociologist whose areas of research specialisation are migration, gender, ethnicity and sexuality. He has published in journals concerned with transnationalism, migration, entrepreneurship, leisure and masculinities and has written book chapters and co-edited books in these areas. Recently he has become involved in research on internationalisation of the curriculum, the attributes of global citizenship, sustainability and transformational learning. He is chair of the Cultural Diversity and Internationalisation Community of Practice at Griffith University in Australia which has conducted symposia on language issues and multi-faith issues in the classroom.

Adrian Holliday

Adrian Holliday is Professor of Applied Linguistics at Canterbury Christ Church University, where he supervises doctoral research in the critical sociology of language education and intercultural communication, and is also the Head of the Graduate School. His publications deal with cultural chauvinism in English language education and the Western ideologies which inhibit our understanding of non-Western cultural realities. Between 1973 and 1976 he was an English teacher in Iran. During the 1980s he set up a language centre at Damascus University, Syria and was a curriculum consultant at Ain Shams University, Cairo, Egypt.

Felix Maringe

Felix Maringe is a senior lecturer in education at the University of Southampton. He teaches and researches on leadership, management, globalisation and internationalisation in higher education. Felix is currently Director of the Centre for Higher Education Management Policy at Southampton (CHEMPaS) and is the chair of the special interest group on Higher Education Marketing of the Academy of Marketing UK.

Patricie Mertova

Patricie Mertova is currently a Research Fellow in the Department of Education, University of Oxford, UK. She was previously a Research Officer at the University of Queensland, and, prior to that, a Research Fellow in the Centre for the Advancement of Learning and Teaching and the Centre for Higher Education Quality, Monash University, Australia. She has recently completed her PhD focusing on the academic voice in higher education quality. She has research expertise in the areas of higher education and higher education quality. Her background is also in the areas of linguistics, translation, cross-cultural communication and foreign languages.

Catherine Montgomery

Catherine Montgomery is Associate Director of the Centre for Excellence in Teaching and Learning at Northumbria University. Her subject background is Sociolinguistics and she is interested in the socio-cultural context of learning in higher education. Catherine was awarded a National Teaching Fellowship in 2010.

John Paul Ndoumin

John Paul Ndoumin is an alumnus of Northumbria University, having graduated with a BA in Contemporary Language Studies and gaining a MA in Conference and Event Management in 2008. John Paul is now a freelance interpreter and translator, working for a range of successful agencies including Sky Sports and a number of Premiership Football Clubs. John Paul has also established community language classes for refugees and asylum seekers in the North East of England.

Claire Sedgwick

Claire Sedgwick is a third-year English Literature student at Northumbria University. She has engaged in voluntary work with the North East Refugee Society establishing creative writing groups for refugees and asylum seekers. As part of this work she has been integral to the production of an anthology of creative writing. Claire is also active in promoting volunteering activities to students in universities across the UK.

Jane Spiro

Jane Spiro is a Principal Lecturer running MA programmes at Oxford Brookes University, UK. Her previous posts include: leading teacher development programmes for Mexican University teachers; Assistant Director of Studies at Pecs University, Hungary; co-ordinator of the English Language Centre at Nottingham University; course manager of teacher training programmes in Switzerland, Poland and the Netherlands. She is the author of Creative Poetry Writing (2004) and Storybuilding (2007) with Oxford University Press, and is a published poet and novelist with a recent PhD and research/teaching commitment to the connections between creative practitioner and educator.

Internalisation of the curriculum for global citizenship in Higher Education

1

Valerie Clifford and Catherine Montgomery

The title of this book 'Internationalisation of the Curriculum for Global Citizenship in Higher Education' reflects a journey that we have travelled over the last three years along with colleagues from around the world. Our approach to internationalising the curriculum (IoC) is a radical rather than a liberal one. It conceives internationalising the curriculum as a 'counterhegemonic educational process' (Schoorman, 2000, p. 2), challenging current course content and pedagogy and offering a transformative educational experience to students. The transformative approach has a very strong agenda of active global citizenship, and we have worked to show our institutions that internationalising the university must include a redevelopment of the curriculum to give all students an education that will equip them to live and work successfully in our globalised world, a movement also known as 'Internationalisation at Home' (Nilsson, 1999). Foregrounding the concept of 'global citizenship' politicises IoC and situates education in the moral terrain of rights and duties. While some argue that there is no 'society' for global citizens to be citizens of, we see 'planet earth' as our commonality (Griffiths, 1998) and endorse the ethic of social justice, where we do not 'secure a better life for [ourselves] at the expense of a much worse life for others' (Wringe, 1999, p. 6). Davies (2006) illustrates the interconnectedness of our lives at all levels by expanding the well used phrase 'act locally, think globally' to 'act local, analyse national and think global' (p. 10), giving as an example the plight of refugees, a global problem, which is responded to by national policies that have local implications.

Many definitions of global citizenship are offered throughout this book: see Caruana, and Barker, Hibbins and Farrelly (this volume). However, a firm understanding of how to develop and implement a radical approach to internationalising the curriculum remains to be developed (Green & Mertova, this volume; Clifford, 2009; Clifford, 2005). Although much work has been done, much more still needs to be done to enhance understanding of what it means and how it might be achieved. Much initial work on internationalising the curriculum involved the 'contribution' and 'additive' approaches (Banks, 1993). The former approach celebrates diversity through such things as festivals, music and food, while the latter involves the adding of case studies from different parts of the world to the curriculum. While such first steps have merit, students themselves challenge the usefulness of these approaches for gaining any real depth of understanding; seeing the examples as too limited and seldom presented in ways that lead to multi-cultural learning (Clifford, 2005). Similarly, the expectation that mixing students from different cultures in the same classroom, or putting them into culturally mixed work groups, will lead to inter-cultural interaction and understanding, often leads to disappointment (Clifford, 2010; Dunne, 2009; Leask, 2009; Turner, 2009).

The critical pedagogy and transformative approach to the curriculum espoused in this book requires universities and staff to engage with paradigmatic change (Gacel-Avil, 2005), a huge intellectual challenge. While the challenge offered to academics by this radical stance has excited some, it has met resistance from others. Some claim that it is irrelevant to their discipline because their discipline is already internationalised (e.g. the worldwide acceptance of current western scientific theory and method), others see their task as limited to developing employable professionals, and others find it just too difficult to challenge their disciplinary canon (Clifford, 2009; Green & Mertova, this volume).

Initially, when working with academic staff, we explained IoC by adopting a framework of global perspectives, intercultural awareness, and responsible citizenship. This allowed individual academics to select a starting point where they might feel comfortable. For some a 'global perspectives' approach of 'adding' an international case study to the curriculum may be a first step, while for others, dealing with issues of cross-cultural communication might be pertinent in their multi-cultural classrooms; while others found an entry by considering the (multi)cultural problems of ensuring a sustainable future for generations to come. In general, while we found that lecturers were often happy to 'tinker around the edges' of their course content and classroom pedagogy, we soon began to realise that the area frequently left unaddressed, and sometimes positively rejected, was that of responsible citizenship (Clifford, 2009; Haigh & Clifford, 2010). It was realised that, to achieve any radical change in curricula, we needed to engage programme teams in taking a step back from their courses, looking at them afresh, and rethinking the educational objectives of their programmes. The challenge for them was to question not only the pedagogy, but also the epistemology and ontology of their disciplines, a shift 'from the comfortable spaces of knowing to the uncomfortable places of learning' (Phillips et al., 2009, p. 1455).

This rethinking of educational objectives also requires a rethink at university level of the purpose of university education. This debate has received some attention with the introduction of the concept of institutional graduate attributes. As universities have taken on the mantle of being 'international' institutions they have begun to talk of developing 'internationalised' students and to write graduate attributes aimed at achieving this. The concept was most fully

developed first by the University of South Australia. Their Graduate
Quality Seven states that a' Graduate of the University of South
Australia demonstrates international perspectives as a professional
and as a citizen' (University of South Australia, 2010). The nine points
that elucidate the meaning of this are mainly couched in the language
of 'valuing', 'recognising' and 'appreciating' and include the
development of an awareness of their own culture and those of
others, a recognition of global perspectives and intercultural issues in
their professional practice, and furthermore a requirement that
graduates 'demonstrate awareness of the implications of local
decisions and actions for international communities and of
international decisions and actions for local communities'. While
these early conceptualisations of an internationalised graduate call for
awareness of implications of actions there is no overt commitment to
issues of social equality, justice and sustainability. Definitions of
internationalised graduates now abound (see Clifford & Haigh in this
book), but evaluation has shown that Australian universities have, so
far, been less than successful in developing the attributes they claim
in their graduates (Barrie, Hughes & Smith, 2009). In their study De
La Harpe et al. (2009, p. iv) concluded 'that teaching and assessing
graduate attributes in an explicit way is a complex, pedagogically
sophisticated task that only a minority, rather than a majority, of
academic staff are able and willing to undertake effectively.'

Both of these movements (of IoC and Graduate Attributes) question
the fundamental rationale for higher education and challenge the
very strong link that has developed between industry and higher
education to produce highly employable graduates to the possible
detriment of a broader education (Haigh, 2008; Barnett, 2006; Hager
& Holland, 2006; Harvey, 2005). Along with this, curricula accredited
by professional associations often lack wider frames of reference, or
knowledge of adapting theory and practice to differing cultural needs.

While the idea of a 'global citizen' is highly contested in some areas we strongly believe that this is a concept that we wish to work with (and work on) and offer the Oxfam (2006) definition as most closely fitting our work. This definition states that a global citizen is someone who:

* is aware of the wider world and has a sense of their own role as a world citizen;
* respects and values diversity;
* has an understanding of how the world works economically, politically, socially, culturally, technologically and environmentally;
* is outraged by social injustice;
* participates in and contributes to the community at a range of levels from local to global;
* is willing to act to make the world a more sustainable place, and;
* takes responsibility for their actions.

It becomes apparent that educating global citizens requires a more holistic philosophy and redevelopment of the curricula. It is important that we start the journey with an awareness of our own underlying assumptions. Schultz (2007, p. 255) offers three contrasting outcomes of different types of global education: the neo-liberal approach, producing individuals in privileged positions to travel and work across national boundaries; the radical approach, which fights to resist globalisation and to strengthen local and national institutions; and the transformative approach, where citizens have an understanding of a common humanity, a shared planet and a shared future. It is the latter stance that is embedded in our ideas of IoC for global citizenship.

The Centre for International Curriculum Inquiry and Networking (CICIN) has held three conferences. Papers from the first conference were published in a double issue of the Journal of Studies in International Education (2009, vol. 13), and the papers from the second conference were published in a special issue of Higher Education Research and Development (2011, vol. 5 issue 3). With the third conference, entitled 'IoC for Global Citizenship: Policy, Practice and Pitfalls' we wanted to construct a coherent narrative on the theme and so choose a book format. This proved very challenging, as peoples' contributions reflected what interested them, what they were doing and what they were thinking. We have created a structure to address theory, policy, research and practice, to reflect emergent work in this area, and to add to the worldwide debate about IoC and global citizenship. Seeking a change in the fundamental orientation of a curriculum provides a challenge not just for academics but also for institutions and disciplines. We hope this book will provide prompts along all these roads.

Our book begins by taking a university-wide look at internationalisation. Felix Maringe's chapter considers the claims by universities worldwide, over the last two decades, to be 'international' institutions, and, more recently the claims of a few to be 'global' institutions. The latter declare that they have 'world class' curricula, pedagogy and research and that they develop 'world class' talent. Felix concludes that few can, currently, claim to be 'global' universities and that to move in this direction requires 'a complete overhaul of the nature and focus of curriculum offered accompanied by an overhaul of the structures and the re-skilling of personnel required to champion the new global reformation in higher education'.

Barker, Hibbins and Farrelly's chapter explores the place of university strategic plans, learning principles and graduate attribute statements for embedding IoC in the institution, with a case study from their own university. They conclude that institutional and senior management support is imperative in advancing IoC, but also that this must be accompanied by professional development for the staff who will be enacting the university policies. It is also essential to involve academics in the creation of the professional development activities, to ensure engagement and re-development of curricula.

In their research Green and Mertova interviewed staff in leadership positions, to investigate the understanding of IoC and responsibility for generating change in the area. They demonstrate the confusion around the ideas of IoC and the lack of clarity about who should be driving this agenda at senior and middle management level. They urge an improvement in this situation, as such a wide reaching change cannot be left to the efforts of lone, energetic individuals.

The final paper in the policy section examines the graduate attribute statements of universities in the UK, Australia and India to glean the vision that the universities hold for the future citizens that they are educating. Clifford and Haigh find a strong focus on developing capable, employable professionals with international perspectives, but less attention given to notions of developing graduates who are responsible, active citizens. This is a concern in a world where choosing to care for each other and for our planet may no longer be an optional alternative.

Having considered IoC from an institutional perspective we now consider what is happening to the curriculum in practice. We have chosen to look at this from a stance of research into our own teaching, in order to encourage and illustrate the variety of current approaches to IoC research, as well as foregrounding the importance of our own self development as the basis of research. Students interviewed in a research project in Australia, Malaysia and South Africa saw staff as the primary critical factor in receiving an internationalised education (Clifford, 2005). They discussed the attributes they saw as necessary for staff which included 'the "willingness and openness" among staff to learn about other cultures and about teaching . . . [and for] the diverse teaching staff and students to share their perspectives' (Clifford, 2010, p. 173). Teekens (2003) and Sanderson (2011) have further explored what this means in terms of professional development. Here Montgomery and Clifford overview the research questions and methodologies in IoC over the last two decades and what this volume offers.

In the first chapter illustrating research and practice, Holliday explores the essentialist views of culture, promulgated by Hofstede (2003) and influencing much of our perceptions of 'others'. He sees us as captured by our own cultural conceptualisations of ourselves and others, and asks how we can engage in critical self analysis such that we move beyond these. He explores this question by showing students behaving against stereotype and using the stereotypes to their advantage.

In the following chapter we present an example of the growth of individual cultural self awareness and engagement in self development. Davis presents a personal reflective journey demonstrating a clear connection between the challenges she faces in her teaching, her own personal 'internationalisation', and how this is informing the enhancement of her curriculum to be more meaningful and relevant to students from diverse cultural backgrounds.

Not only do we need to think differently, we also need to learn to research differently and find new ways of expressing, not only our ideas, but also our emotional reactions, which are an intrinsic part of the dynamics of reflection (Mällki, 2010). Montgomery and Spiro use the medium of poetry to stimulate deep thought and revelations about life-changing experiences, tapping into a different level of reaction and thought.

Next we move to exploring the possibilities for generating activism through the curriculum. Montgomery introduces us to three students who initiated volunteer involvement themselves and tell us how it has enhanced their understanding of their studies and of the persons they wish to become. They argue cogently that such experiences should not sit outside the curriculum but should be a critical part of it.

Finally Caruana defines global citizenship as based on 'the cornerstone principles of participation, responsibility and activism'. She argues that universities may well produce graduates who are 'cosmopolitan' but who are not 'global citizens' as the essential ingredient of activism is missing from their education. She believes that service learning and volunteerism provide the means of introducing the elements of participation, responsibility and activism into the formal and informal curriculum.

Through this book we offer a way into the complex debates on IoC and global citizenship education, and provide examples of IoC for global citizenship at work in policy, research and practice. We hope that it inspires you to join us on this journey, along with your colleagues, to explore creative ways to engage with, and take forward, these ideas. We hope you enjoy reading this book, and any of the authors would welcome further discussion with you.

References

Banks, J.A. (1993). Approaches to multi-cultural reform. In J.A. Banks & C.A.M. Banks (Eds.), *Multicultural education: issues and perspectives*. Boston: Allyn and Bacon.

Barnett, R. (2006). Graduate Attributes in an age of uncertainty. In S. Holland & P. Hager, *Graduate Attributes, Learning and Employability* (pp. 49–65). Dordrecht: Springer.

Barrie, S., Hughes, C. & Smith, C. (2009). *Report. The national graduate attributes project: integration and assessment of graduate attributes in curriculum.* Australian Learning and Teaching Council Ltd with Australian Government Department of Education, Employment and Workplace Relations. Retrieved March 21, 2011, from **http://www.altc.edu.au/resources?text=barrie**

Clifford, V.A. (2010). Ch 13 The Internationalised curriculum: (dis)locating students. In E. Jones (Ed.), *Internationalisation and the Student Voice* (pp. 169–180). London: Routledge.

Clifford, V.A. (2009). Engaging the Disciplines in Internationalising the Curriculum, *International Journal of Academic Development, 14*(2), 133–143.

Clifford, V.A. (2005). Embracing and resisting border pedagogies: student views of internationalising the curriculum in higher education. In A. Brew & C. Asmar (Eds.), *Higher Education in a Changing World. Research and Development in Higher Education, vol 28,* (pp. 116–123). Retrieved March 20, 2011 from **http://www.herdsa.org.au/wp-content/uploads/conference/2005/papers/clifford.pdf**

Davies, L. (2006). Global citizenship: abstraction or framework for action? *Educational Review, 58*(1), 5–25.

De la Harpe, B., David, C., Dalton, H., Thomas, J. & Girardi, A. (2009). *The b factor project. Understanding academic staff beliefs about graduate attributes. Final report 2009.* Australian Learning and Teaching Council Ltd with Australian Government Department of Education, Employment and Workplace Relations. Retrieved March 21, 2011 from **http://www.altc.edu.au/resources?text=de+la+harpe**

Dunne, C. (2009). Host Students' Perspectives of Intercultural Contact in an Irish University. *Journal of Studies in International Education, 13,* 222–239.

Gacel-Ávila, J. (2005). The Internationalisation of Higher Education: A Paradigm for Global Citizenry. *Journal of Studies in International Education, 9*(2), 121–136.

Griffith, R. (1998). *Educational citizenship and independent learning.* London: Jerssica Kingsley.

Hager, P., & Holland, S. (2006). Introduction. In P. Hager & S. Holland (Eds.), *Graduate attributes, learning and employability* (pp. 1–15). Dordrecht: Springer.

Haigh, M. 2008. Internationalisation, Planetary Citizenship and Higher Education Inc. *Compare: A Journal of Comparative Education, 38*(4), 427–449.

Haigh, M. & Clifford, V. (2010). Widening the Graduate Attribute Debate: a Higher Education for Global Citizenship. *Brookes electronic Journal of Learning and Teaching, 2*(5). Retrieved February 15, 2011 from **http://bejlt.brookes.ac.uk/article/widening_the_graduate_attribute _debate_a_higher_education_for_global_citize/**

Harvey, L. (2005). Embedding and integrating employability. *New Directions for Institutional Research,* 128, 13–28.

Hofstede, G. (2003). *Culture's consequences: comparing values, behaviours, institutions and organizations across cultures* (2nd ed.). London: Sage.

Leask, B. (2009). Using formal and informal curricula to improve interactions between home and international students. *Journal of Studies in International Education, 13,* 205–221.

Mällki, K. (2010). Building on Mezirow's theory of transformative lerarning: theorising the challenges to reflection. *Journal of Transformative Education, 8*(1), 42–62.

Nilsson, B. (1999). Internationalisation at home – theory and praxis. *EAIE Forum,* Spring, 12.global levels. Development Education Journal, 6, 4–6.

Oxfam Development Education Program (2006). *Education for global citizenship: a guide for schools.* Retrieved December 26, 2010 from **http://www.oxfam.org.uk/education/gc/files/education_for_global _citizenship_a_guide_for_schools.pdf**

Phillips, D. K., Harris, G., Larson, M.L. & Higgins, K. (2009). Trying on-being in-becoming. Four women's journey(s) in feminist poststructural theory. *Qualitative Inquiry, 15*(9), 1455–1479.

Sanderson, G. (2011). Internationalisation and teaching in higher education. *Special Issue Internationalising the Home Student, Higher Education Research and Development, 30*(5) in press.

Schoorman, D. (2000). What really do we mean by 'internationalization'. *Contemporary Education, 71*(4), 1–13.

Shultz, L. (2007). Educating for global citizenship: conflicting agendas and understandings. *Alberta Journal of Educational Research, 53*(3). 248–258.

Teekens, H. (2003). The requirement to develop specific skills for teaching in an intercultural setting. *Journal of Studies in International Education, 7*(1), 108–119.

Turner, Y. (2009). 'Knowing me knowing you'. Is there nothing we can do? Pedagogic challenges in using group work to create an intercultural learning space. *Journal of Studies in International Education, 13*, 240–255.

University of South Australia (2010). *Indicators of graduate qualities.* Retrieved March 16, 2011 from **http://www.unisa.edu.au/gradquals/staff/indicators.asp**

Wringe, C. (1999). Issues in citizenship at national, local and global levels. *Development Education Journal, 6*, 4–6.

Part 1

Policy

Higher Education transitions: from international to global institutions

2

Felix Maringe

Abstract

This chapter explores the declaration of some universities to be 'global' institutions, differentiating themselves from the now pervasive claim to be 'international'. Results of an internet search and a global survey of the impact of globalisation on universities are used to posit four figural elements (of place, prominence, programme and product), in the transition from international to global.

Introduction

For more than twenty years, universities across the world have used Jane Knight's concept of international universities as places where an effort was being made to integrate an international dimension into universities' traditional purposes of teaching research and service (Knight, 2004). The extent to which universities could demonstrate sufficient integration in these areas became a benchmark for university quality and international standing in the higher education league tables (Taylor, 2010; Foskett, 2010).

More recently the term 'global university' has come into use, a bold statement of intent and a means by which leading universities seek to ie for themselves to stand out prominently in the ıarketplace (Woodfield, Middlehurst and Fielden, 2009). In ess world, global businesses (e.g. Coca-Cola, Nike, Sony) emer. ı because they saw opportunities in multiple markets across the world which could be served essentially by the provision of a standard product, ensuring the advantages of economies of scale, lower costs, faster production and distribution and cheaper marketing (Porter, 1996). On the other hand there are multi-domestic business organisations which are decentralised and based on differentiated strategies for varied markets. Many universities tend to fall into this second category, although there are now a few examples of universities that are developing their global strategies along the global industry model. Examples of the latter in the UK include Liverpool and Nottingham Universities, which have established campuses in China and Malaysia respectively; and in Australia, Monash has campuses in Malaysia and South Africa. Some American schools have established 'semester abroad' facilties in the Gulf and other parts of the Middle East.

Although there is a growing literature on the nature of the global university (Marginson, 2010; Maringe & Foskett, 2010) the concept is still largely underdeveloped. This chapter explores this concept by researching the differences between universities that claim to be international and those that claim to be global, and by considering the transformations take place in universities that are going global.

To address these questions, the chapter begins by reviewing the notion of globalisation and how universities are currently responding to this in their mission statements and their associated strategies. It then draws on the results of a survey, responded to by a range of universities across the world, to explore understandings of a 'global university'. From these findings four figural elements emerge as characterising global universities.

The response of higher education to globalisation

Globalisation has been a key influence of the late 20th and early 21st centuries and has to all intents and purposes replaced postmodernism as a lens for examining, analysing, interpreting and understanding society and social processes (Maringe and Foskett, 2010). As a concept, globalisation is a complex and multifaceted idea with political/ideological, socio-cultural, economic and technological dimensions driving change in societies across the world (Steger, 2003). Although globalisation is highly contested and elicits diverse responses from different people, ranging from those seeing it as an inevitable force for the good of humanity to those who see it as a contrived programme designed to entrench western domination in all spheres of human endeavour (Steger, 2003; Maringe & Foskett, 2010), globalisation has had fundamental impact on the lives of people across the world. In very broad terms, globalisation is closely associated with the following world developments.

First is the domination of market forces as the key driver of the world's economic engines based on Keynesian concepts of supply and demand. In higher education, market forces which currently reflect depressed economic performance are driving governments to consider reduced spending and funding cuts to universities and in the process influencing supply and demand factors in the sector (Richardson, 2010).

Second is the increase in human migration due to improved transport standards, increasing world economic and poverty differentials, human conflict and widely different standards of living in different parts of the world. In higher education it is estimated that currently there are some three million students studying outside their home countries, and the figure is estimated to increase to eight million by 2015 (International Development Programme, 2007).

Third is the increasing speed of human communication accelerated by the internet and broadband. This has had profound impact on the way decisions are made both in business and in education and has also contributed significantly to increased uptake of distance learning opportunities and in the dissemination of knowledge in general (Salmi, 2005). Associated with this is the fourth element of increasing social and cultural integration of societies, including language use and the increasing dominance of English. Although only a fifth of the world use English as the official language of business and commerce, more than 75% of universities across the world teach in English. Mydans (2004) proclaimed that English was the language of globalisation and that its spread across the world, while facilitating business communication and decisions, would threaten local cultures and languages in a very real sense.

In the UK globalisation is associated with the increasing internationalisation of educational institutions, both in terms of increasing human diversity in the sector, real changes to the curriculum taught, and the transformation of learning spaces, making universities international in outlook and in essence. Also there is the coming together of world educational systems being facilitated by comparisons of world systems: for example, the Programme for International Students Assessment sponsored by the OECD (2009), and Trends in Mathematics and Science Studies (International Education Statistics, 2007), both designed to gather data about comparative performances of educational systems across the world. In the field of leadership and management, the GLOBE project (House et al 2004) gathers evidence from 62 countries which is used to analyse the relationship between culture, organisational culture and leadership practice and values.

Finally, world education systems are increasingly coming under the influence of international organisations. For example, in Europe the European Union, through the Bologna protocol, has a substantial voice in educational policy for countries in the union. In Southern Africa, the South African Development Community (2010) has an overarching policy for educational and economic development for the region, while the Economic Community of West African Countries (2010) oversees the policy framework for West African countries. The United Nations, through the Millennium Development Goals (2010), tends to exert global influence on a range of policy issues especially those relating to participation and equity of educational provision.

As mentioned above, the definition of internationalisation that has been used across the tertiary sector in a number of western countries over the last two decades is that of Knight (2004), who saw it as a process of integration of an international dimension into the teaching, research and service elements of the university. This definition emphasises the international rather than the global, but perhaps has been taken up by universities because of the inference that internationalisation should be embedded in all aspects of universities. By 2007, internationalisation had become one of the key strategic ambitions of many universities across the world (Ayoubi and Massoud, 2007). Studies have shown that the term 'international' has become the strategic concept of choice in the mission statements of universities in different parts of the world (Maringe, 2009; Ayoubi & Massoud 2007; Foskett, 2010; Taylor 2010).

International: the 21st Century Strategy of Choice in Higher Education

An internet search of the mission statements of 84 university websites in the major regions of the world (Maringe, 2009) identified that the most frequently used idea for describing the overarching ambition of the university was the notion of being international. The majority of the universities (63/84) aspired to become international centres of excellence while a significant number (47/84) described themselves essentially as leading centres of international excellence in research and teaching. One UK university expresses its mission as follows:

> We are committed to further improve our position as a leading research university of international standing, distinguished by our enterprise. We aspire to be a place of opportunity and inspiration that attracts talented staff and students regardless of their background. By 2015 we expect to be measurably recognisable as a successful, influential, international university that has both strong roots in its locality and a substantial global presence. (University of Southampton Ambition and Strategic Aim, 2010).

It can be argued that this university sets its ambition in a transitional mode, sure about its commitment to the local environment but equally ambitious about its desire to be a global institution. Maringe and Foskett (2010) have described such universities as Glocal universities. Similarly the University of London defines its strategic vision as follows:

> The university will continue to be acknowledged both nationally and internationally for its excellence in academic achievement (University of London, 2009).

Finally, being international and being seen as international needs to be supported by a range of strategies and these may include the following:

* increasing the share of international students on campus;
* increasing the share of international staff on university programmes;
* promoting growth of university talent through collaborative and partnership development programmes in teaching, research and enterprise;

* supporting staff and student mobility to gain and develop international awareness, skills and competences;

* developing joint degree programmes with carefully selected strategic partners;

* developing overseas campuses to export the educational and research programme;

* internationalising the institutional, programme and subject teaching curricula;

* developing international reach and presence through increased distance teaching and learning.

International university league tables such as the Times Higher Education (THE) world rankings and the Shanghai Jiao Tong University (SJTU) have increasingly been highlighting the above criteria as measures of university performance. The THE have allocated 10% of the total scores on their rankings to performance criteria related to number of international students and staff. Another key criterion for international status is the number of publications on the Science Citation and Social Science Citation Indices with international joint authorship (Batty, 2010). While these measures are contentious, they nevertheless provide some way of comparing areas of internationalisation in university institutions and programmes.

The Global Survey of the Impact of Globalisation in Universities (Maringe and Foskett, 2009)

To further explore the perception of the impact of internationalisation and globalisation on universities across the world, a self-report questionnaire was developed at the University of Southampton and administered to 200 randomly selected universities in the major regions of the world, including North America and Canada, South America, Africa, the Middle East, Asia and the Pacific region, China, Japan and the Koreas. After three data sweeps 51 responses were obtained, giving a

25% response rate. Alreck and Settle (1995) have shown that response rates of 5 to 20% are most common in questionnaire surveys. As such, it is often assumed that a 15% + response rate provides for a valid extrapolation/generalisation into the entire population. We cannot claim absolute representativeness of the responses but have the confidence that all major regions of world were represented in the data. The questionnaire sought to determine the following from each of the participating universities among other things:

* Universities' understanding of what it meant to be a global university;
* How global universities differed from those with an international focus;
* How individual universities were responding to the global influence;
* Strategies used by universities to strengthen their global competitiveness.

Questions included Likert type and open-ended items to get both quantitative and qualitative data.

An example of a Likert type question was:

> On a scale of 1 to 5, indicate how important the following strategies for strengthening the global competitiveness of your university are in your own university: international students recruitment; international staff recruitment; curriculum internationalisation; development of international research partnerships; development of offshore teaching; development of distance learning programmes; development of strong alumni relations; development of university/employer collaborative activity; development of institutional partnerships with global organisations; rebranding our institution.

An example of an open-ended question was:

> Indicate in the space below why your university describes
> itself as an international or as a global centre of excellence.

Survey results

The survey responses fell into three broad areas around the emerging
concept of the global university. First is an indication of the extent
and context of use of the idea of a global university among the
universities surveyed. Second, are the organisational aspects that
characterise these global focused universities? And thirdly, were some
key transitional strategies for universities seeking to become global
rather than just international institutions?

On being a global university

Respondents to the global survey were asked to define their
understanding of the concepts of internationalisation and
globalisation and to explain the missions of their universities in the
context of these ideas. All universities that participated in the survey
related with the idea of being international institutions. For most, the
notion of being international was closely associated with concepts
such as: opening up programmes to people from all corners of the
world; programmes that were taught by top talent from different parts
of the world; programmes that reflected high levels of international
content/relevance; involvement in offshore teaching programmes;
collaborative activity with international partners in research and
teaching; having international partnership with strategically selected
institutions; and developing strategic and operational presence in
fertile higher education recruitment markets.

Only a handful of old well-established universities located mostly in
rich western countries, and consistently found in the top 200 of world

university rankings, made some strong and bold statements that positioned them as global universities. For example in one such UK university, its ambition was expressed as:

> By 2015 we expect to be measurably recognisable as a successful, influential, international university that has both strong roots in its locality and a substantial global presence.

Another UK university in London which has consistently been in the top 10 of world rankings positions itself as a global university and has clear strategy for attracting only the best students from all walks of life across the world. In a USA university, the global ambition is expressed in terms of the power of world-leading research and as being a place where ideas are created and challenged and where human minds are transformed into world-class talent. However, other universities outside the traditional top ten also espouse global or international ambitions. Here we have to distinguish between ambition and reality. A relatively small new university in Southern Africa has a mission to become an eminently global university, while another fairly well established university in Germany has a mission to be recognised as a truly global university of the highest standing. While such universities could pass as international institutions, they may not necessarily be classified as global universities by their peers, nor in relation to our emerging definition of a global university.

Universities declaring themselves to be global also made bold statements referring to the acquisition of world-class talent, a few having clear ambitions to attract and retain a number of Nobel prize winners by 2015. Some also have statements of support for exceptional talent through substantial scholarship schemes for students from the developing world.

The organisational characteristics of globally focused universities

Universities which expressed global ambitions tended to have a number of organisational aspects dedicated to this ambition. There were often appointments at Vice President / Deputy Vice Chancellor / Pro Vice Chancellor level with specific responsibility for an international portfolio and an explicit global strategy. These portfolios often come with relatively large budgets to support the international activity of the university, including senior management travel on global assignments. There is often a high profile centre dedicated to some aspects of global significance, e.g. Centre for the Study of Global Terrorism; Centre for the Study of Global Climate Change; Centre for Control of World Communicable Diseases. Some of the universities host prestigious international chairs, e.g. the UNESCO Chair for the study of world peace; UNESCO chair for the comparative study of world religions. Commercial recruitment companies are frequently employed to identify, recruit and develop employment packages designed to attract and retain world-class talent. The institutions also have an underlying culture that stresses the global ambition of the university in very explicit terms.

Transitional strategies for moving from international to global university

Being a global brand in higher education appears to be associated with both static and dynamic variables. For example, chances of becoming a global brand outside of the location of a big global city appear to be minimal. So too are chances of suddenly earning a tradition which only comes with years and years of existence as a university. However, other variables tend to be more malleable, in that institutions can positively influence how they can play to the strengths associated with those variables.

The intellectual ambition of global universities is very bold and unequivocal. Some do not shy away from describing themselves as elite institutions which only admit people of exceptional ability from all corners of the world. Ability or inability to pay is not the criterion for joining the ranks of the university. The only criterion that matters is intellectual capability. Other global universities situate themselves as the prime resource for developing leadership in global institutions. Between them, Oxford, Harvard, Chicago, Cambridge and MIT are said to have produced 75% of Nobel Prize laureates and 45% of the world's leaders of stable democracies (Smith, 2010). The intellectual ambition stated by some UK universities in terms of recruiting the most cited academics in different fields, bringing Nobel prize laureates to the staff of the university, and admitting only the most gifted students from different parts of the world have become the strategies of choice for transforming the prominence of universities.

The product of the university can be its graduates; its high-impact programmes such as partnerships for collaborative research and teaching; its enterprise activity and spin-out companies; its intellectual capital in terms of theses output and research publications; its place in the knowledge community as a resource for consultancy work. Work around global graduate attributes is helping some universities to enhance their global competitiveness, while the creation of university partnerships with strategically selected institutions and organisations is gradually becoming the strategy of choice for enhancing the global profile of universities (Foskett, 2010). Universities seeking high-impact outcomes tend to have very clear strategies for raising the publications profiles of individuals and of the university. This involves contracting staff to publications targets in designated publishing outlets. For example the University of Cape Town, the only university in Africa which is consistently in the top 200 on world university league tables, promotes only those staff who have published with any of a small list of prestigious publishers. University spin-out companies are formed on the back of academic research owned by specific universities. For example, the University of Oxford has generated over £260 million from spin-out companies since 2000 (ISIS Innovation Group, 2009). Part of this money is ploughed back into the university to further develop the research, stimulate local economic development and create jobs both on campus and in the local area.

Discussion

It is clear that many universities across the world have clear ambitions about being international institutions. Only a few have made bold intentions to break away from the pack and declare themselves global universities. While our work has shown the clearly stated intentions of these latter universities in terms of their strategies, organisational structures and funding priorities, and their vision of stocking the university with world-class talent, the universities may also need to consider the changing demographic of students and the extent of curricular change they need to promote. In order to illustrate ways of moving towards being a global university, this section will consider a model that indicates the areas that a university may need to focus on. (Figure 1 overleaf)

Ivy's work (2008) on the marketing of higher education drew out seven important elements, four of which appear figural in the transition to being a global university: those of place, prominence, programme and product.

Many universities were built for a traditional undergraduate male-dominated market of young people age 19–25 (Arambewela & Maringe, 2010). That demography is hardly recognisable today. Under globalisation, universities have become demographically and culturally diverse places of study with more international students and staff than was the case ten years ago (Altbach, 2006). The universities' growth of postgraduate programmes is also attracting a

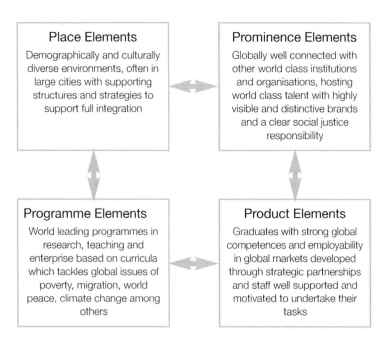

Figure 1: Key features of the global university (Adapted from work by Ivy, 2008)

different demographic of mature students. Fundamentally, the 'place' elements (Ivy, 2008) of universities looking to becoming global institutions will require radical transformation with structural, systemic and organisational aspects focused on the wider needs of the global community of the university.

The programme elements (Ivy, 2008) of the university are encapsulated in its curriculum. It has been argued that despite the curriculum being the mainstay of universities, it is the one that university personnel (especially academics) least want to change. Reasons for this include that academics feel disempowered by curriculum change, as they have to invest in relearning new ideas and approaches (Beane, 1997; Stodolsky & Grossman, 1995). Tinkering with the curriculum by mere integration of an international dimension is unlikely to be a sufficient criterion for developing the global curriculum which will have at its core a deliberate element of interrogating issues of global significance. Global universities will need to position themselves as places where ideas about societal development are generated, explored and critiqued. Another area for programme transformation will be the creation of strong collaborations with international organisations such as the WHO, UNESCO, UNICEF and the World Bank, including global companies, as partners in developing the educational programme of the university. The idea of university as a secret garden (Hartley, 2008; Davies, Williams & Webb, 1997) where academics work in isolation is now completely outdated, and needs to be replaced by a new public ownership of intellectual property where multiplicity of perspectives and shared ownership and development of knowledge become valued over the private processes of intellectual transformation in higher education.

While students may apply to proclaimed 'global' universities on the promise and hope of becoming influenced intellectually by world-class talent and transformative curricula, they may be disappointed if they find traditional curricula and non-research staff teaching them. It may be necessary for universities claiming to be global to make sure their high-profile academics have some dedicated teaching, but at the same time employ part-time staff and postgraduate students to support these academics to free up the time for high-profile research. The work being done by some universities to develop programmes which address global citizenship requirements can contribute significantly to the global value and capital of such universities.

Concluding Comments

The focus of internationalisation in Higher Education has delivered qualitative improvements in universities in many significant ways. Universities in general have developed expanded horizons in areas such as international recruitment of students and staff; they have deparochialised their social mission to embrace heightened responsibility for global rather than local issues; and they have also begun to integrate the idea of internationalisation as a substantial element of the quality criteria in universities. Above all, much seems to have been done both in terms of research and in practice to enhance the quality of the international experience of students on university campuses.

It has, however, been argued that striving to become an international university is no longer a sufficient ambition in the context of the global world. Becoming a global player in the higher education sector means seeking to break away from the ordinary mantra of internationalisation which has been the staple diet of contemporary universities in the last two or three decades. It implies a complete refocusing of the mission and purpose of the university. Being a global university seems to require a complete overhaul of the nature and focus of curriculum offered, accompanied by an overhaul of the structures and the re-skilling of personnel required to champion the new global reformation in higher education. But this is not a journey for the faint-hearted. It requires an institutional boldness that seeks not just mere integration of international dimensions into the tripartite mission of universities in teaching, research and service, but redefinition of the purpose of the university and a commitment to be a partner with other global institutions in the interrogation of world issues, problems and challenges. This chapter has presented one model of how universities could start this process by redefining their mission in the four areas of place, programmes, prominence and product elements of university transformation.

References

Alreck, P.L & Settle, R.B. (1995). *Survey research handbook: guidelines and strategies for conducting a survey.* New York: McGraw-Hill.

Altbach, P. (2006). *Globalisation and the university: Realities in an unequal world, Springer International Handbooks on Education.* Vol 18. Netherlands: Springer.

Arambewela, R. & Maringe, F. (2010). International post graduate students experience in a UK University: Lessons for academic practice. In M. Devlin, J. Nagy & A. Lichtenberg (Eds.) *Research and Development in Higher Education, Reshaping Higher Education* (pp. 29–38). 33rd HERDSA Annual Conference, Melbourne.

Ayoubi, R.M. & Massoud, H.K. (2007). The strategy of internationalisation in universities. A quantitative evaluation of the intent and implementation in UK universities. *International Journal of Educational Management.* 21(4), 329–349.

Batty, P. (2010, March). *League Tables. Flawed rankings or key benchmarks.* Paper presented at the Going Global Conference, London.

Beane, J. (1997). *Curriculum Integration.* Teachers College Press: New York.

Davies, P., Williams, J. & Webb, S. (1997). Access to Higher Education in the Late Twentieth Century, Policy, Power and Discourse. In J. Williams (Ed.), *Negotiating access to Higher Education* (pp. 3–18), Buckingham: SRHE/Open University Press.

Economic Community of West African Countries (ECOWAS) (2010). Retrieved February 20, 2010 from **http://www.ecowas.int/**

Foskett, N. (2010). Global markets, national challenges, local strategies: The strategic challenge of internationalisation. In F. Maringe & N. Foskett (Eds.), *Globalisation and internationalisation of higher education, theoretical, strategic and management perspectives* (pp. 35–50). London: Continuum.

Foskett, N. H. & Hemsley-Brown, J. V. (2001). *Choosing Futures: Young people's decision-making in education, training and careers markets.* London: Routledge/Falmer.

Hartley, D. (2008). Education, markets and the pedagogy of personalisation, *British Journal of Educational Studies*, 56(4) 365–381.

Hesketh, A. J. & Knight, P. T. (1999). Postgraduates' choice of programme: helping universities to market and postgraduates to choose. *Studies in Higher Education*, 24(2), 151–163.

House, R.J., Hanges, P.J., Javidan, M., Dorfman, P.W., Gupta, V. & Associates (eds.) (2004) *Culture, leadership and organizations, the Globe study of 62 societies*. Thousand Oaks, CA: Sage.

International Development Program Education Pty Ltd. (2007). *Global Student Mobility: An Australian Perspective Five Years on*. Australia: IDP Education Pty Ltd.

International Education Statistics (2007). *Trends in international mathematics and science study (TIMSS)*, Retrieved February 20, 2010 from **http://nces.ed.gov/timss/**

ISIS Innovation Group (2009). *Annual Report*. Retrieved November 20, 2010 from **http://www.isis-innovation.com/documents/IsisAnnualReport2009.pdf**

Ivy J (2008). A new higher education marketing mix: the 7Ps for MBA marketing. *International Journal of Educational Management*, 22(4): 288–299.

Ivy, J. (2001). Higher Education institution image: a correspondence analysis approach. *International Journal of Educational Management*, 15(6), 276–282.

Knight, J. (2004). Internationalisation remodelled, definitions, approaches and rationale. *Journal of Studies in International Education*, 8(1), 5–31.

Marginson, S. (2010, March). *World potential: Making education meet the challenge*. Opening session of the Going Global Conference London.

Maringe, F. & Foskett, N. (2009). Global survey of the impact of globalisation in universities, a research project developed at the University of Southampton UK. In F. Maringe & N. Foskett, (Eds.) *Globalisation and internationalisation of higher education, theoretical, strategic and management perspectives* (pp. 29–33). London: Continuum

Maringe, F. & Foskett, N. (2010). (Eds.) *Globalisation and internationalisation of higher education, theoretical, strategic and management perspectives.* London: Continuum.

Maringe, F. (2009). Strategies and challenges of internationalisation in higher education: an exploratory study of UK Universities. *International Journal of Educational Management, 23(7),* 553–573.

Mydans, S. (2004, October 3). A World Empire by Other Means English Becoming The New World Language, *The Economist,* Retrieved November 20, 2010 from **http://www.antimoon.com/forum/2004/5712.htm**

OECD, (2009). *Programme for International Student Assessment.* Retrieved February 20, 2010 from **http://www.pisa.oecd.org/pages/0,3417,en_32252351_32235907_1 _1_1_1,00.html**

Porter, M. (1996). *Competition in Global Industries.* New York: Harvard Business School, Harvard.

Richardson, H. (2010, February 1) University Budget cuts revealed, BBC Retrieved February 2, 2010 from **http://news.bbc.co.uk/1/hi/education/8491729.stm**

Salmi, J. (2005). *The capacity building challenge in developing countries; Role and importance of tertiary education and research.* World Bank paper. Retrieved November 22, 2010 from **http://mt.educarchile.cl/mt/jjbrunner/archives/Salmi.pdf**

Smith, L. (2010). *Nobel Laureates and Institutional Affiliations,* Retrieved February 20, 2010 from **http://nobelprize.org**

Southern African Development Community (SADC) (2010). *Towards a common future.* Retrieved February 20, 2010 at **http://www.sadc.int/sadc2010**

Steger, M.B. (2003). *Globalisation, a very short introduction.* Oxford: Oxford University Press.

Stodolsky, S. S. & Grossman, P. A. (1995). The Impact of Subject Matter on Curricular Activity: An Analysis of Five Academic Subjects, *American Educational Research Journal.* 32(2), 227–249.

Taylor, J. (2010). The responses of governments and universities to the internationalisation in higher education. In F. Maringe & N. Foskett (Eds.), *Globalisation and internationalisation of higher education, theoretical, strategic and management perspectives*. (pp. 83–90). London: Continuum.

United Nations, (2010). *We can end poverty. Millenium development goals 2015. United Nations summit 20–22 September*, 2010. Retrieved February 20, 2011 from **http://www.un.org/en/mdg/summit2010/**

University of London, (2009.) *Strategic Plan 2009–2014*. Retrieved April 20, 2010 from **http://www.london.ac.uk/5.html**

University of Southampton (2010). *Ambition and strategic aims*. Retrieved April 29, 2010 from **http://www.resource1.soton.ac.uk/strategy/initiatives/index.html**

Woodfield, S. Middlehurst R. & Fielden J. (2009). *Universities and international higher education partnerships: making a difference*. London: Million+.

Walking the talk: Fostering a sense of global citizenry amongst staff in Higher Education

3

Michelle Barker, Raymond Hibbins
and Brona Farrelly

Abstract

Two interrelated questions challenging higher education today are: what constitutes global citizenship; and how can it be fostered amongst staff? Interestingly, discussion to date has focused predominantly on the need to develop graduates who can demonstrate the qualities of a global citizen. Less attention, however, has been paid to the complex issues faced by higher education institutions in relation to achieving global citizenship education and whether this is synonymous with an internationalised curriculum. In particular, there is a critical need to find evidence-based professional development strategies that enable academic staff themselves to develop the attributes of global citizens.

This chapter presents a case study of the strategy currently implemented in an Australian university to assist staff to 'walk the talk' in relation to global citizenship. This university adopts a 'top down' strategy to global citizenship education, which is demonstrated in the degree to which it is emphasised in the University's strategic plan, learning principles, and graduate attribute statements. Further academic staff are required to use a curriculum review tool \
on the extent to which their students learn to be competent

culturally diverse and international environments. The case study highlights the importance of using an integrated, institution-wide strategy which starts with the end in mind: namely, to help staff develop graduates who have a global and international perspective on their disciplines, as well as being able to demonstrate awareness, knowledge and skills needed to interact effectively in culturally or linguistically diverse contexts. Limitations of the strategy are addressed, particularly in relation to how to diffuse the change agenda with overstretched academic staff who do not recognise global citizenship education as a priority.

While the approach to global citizenship education highlighted in the case study has some important strengths, it is argued that institutions must make a significant investment at both the institutional and grassroots levels to help staff to 'walk the talk' of global citizenship education.

Context Setting

In industry as well as higher education, discussions about the implications of increased global mobility, global crises, and the pervasive reach of multinational organisations heighten the need for competent and interculturally capable citizens (Brownlie, 2001; Bryant, 2006; Falk, 1993; Hanson, 2010; Holden, 2000; Ibrahim, 2005; Nussbaum, 2002; Ramburuth & Welch, 2005; Roman, 2003; Schweisfurth, 2006; Susnowitz, 2009; Tarrant & Sessions, 2008). There is a growing recognition that graduates must demonstrate not only the knowledge and skills required for their chosen career, but the requisite capacities to perform in a society characterised by diversity, rapid social, economic, and environmental change – what Barnett (1998, p. 48) terms 'a constellation of fragility'.

Various discourses can be used to explain motivations for internationalisation, specifically in the tertiary education sector

(Caruana, 2007). The 'marketisation' discourse sees universities vying for international students in an increasingly competitive environment scarred by the globe's current financial crisis. In this top-down, internally-focused model, students are seen as clients, and the internationalisation agenda is based more on revenue creation and technical observance of policies and strategies that purport to achieve internationalisation. An alternative is the 'knowledge economy and learning society' discourse (Caruana & Hanstock, 2005). In this conceptualisation, internationalisation policies focus on the need to graduate socially responsible students who are interculturally competent and capable of negotiating the realities of a world characterised by rapid social, environmental and technical change. The latter, more student-centred discourse is increasingly gaining momentum in the tertiary education sector, especially under the interrelated conceptualisations of 'internationalisation at home' and global citizenship. The implications of these more recent conceptualisations of internationalisation on the choices made regarding professional development of staff are discussed later in this paper.

Turning to Australia, it can be argued that the internationalisation of education has gone through three distinct phases, in which different internationalisation policy motivations have emerged. We have classified these phases as social-, market- and student outcomes-oriented. These phases fit into Hanson's model of internationalisation, which outlines three distinct motivations for internationalisation; market, liberal and social transformation (Hanson, 2010). These will be discussed in turn below.

Social orientation 1950s – 1970s

In the Australian context, it is interesting to note that the initial motivations for the internationalisation of tertiary education came from a foreign aid plan, known as the 'Colombo Plan', which provided scholarship opportunities for educational and cultural exchange, with the goal of improving bilateral relations between Australia and South and South-East Asia. This program heralded the diversification of the education system, and was a landmark development, signalling the move away from the 'white Australia policy' (Oakman, 2002). The diversification of the student population was furthered in the 1980s, when educational reforms led to a shift in policy towards "equity and access for all" (McKenzie & Schweitzer, 2001, p. 21). This policy shift meant that increasing numbers of domestic students from diverse socio-cultural backgrounds were offered opportunities previously unavailable to them to undertake higher education. This first step in the internationalisation and diversification of the tertiary education system falls into what Hanson classifies as a 'social transformation' model, wherein the emphasis is on cross-cultural understanding and on catering to the needs of marginalised groups (Hanson, 2010).

Market orientation 1980s – 2000s

The shift in policy which occurred in the 1980s mirrored a shift in how universities were perceived. Rather than being conceptualised as state-owned institutions characterised by their scholarly and academic pursuits, Australian universities began to be seen more as businesses, within a corporate-enterprise model. The latter involved a focus on catering to the needs of the market (students as consumers) as universities became increasingly commercialised (Lynch, 2009; McInnis, 1995). During the 'market' orientation stage, international student enrolments increased rapidly and this sector continues to provide a significant source of revenue for Australian universities. Figures from March 2010 indicate that there were 432,678 enrolments by full-fee international visa students in Australia, representing growth of 5.9% within a 1 month period. On average, there has been an annual growth rate of 11.1% in international student enrolments since 2002 (AEI, 2010). This rapid growth has led to a further change in policy regarding internationalisation. According to Hanson's (2010) 'market model', internationalisation is primarily concerned with improving the competitive advantage of universities through the recruitment of fee paying international students. At the same time, the Australian student population became increasingly diversified in terms of their cultural and linguistically diverse (CALD) backgrounds (Coates & Krause, 2005).

Student outcomes orientation 2000s – present

Resulting from the changes discussed above was recognition of the need to provide students with competencies and skills which are transferrable across a range of cultural contexts. This stage of the internationalisation process is not only based on institutional processes of universities competing for international students, but also on recognition of the need to provide educational processes which will help prepare all students for a globalised work environment. This model is closely related to the 'productive diversity' policy pursued by the Australian government in the late 1990s. The focus here is on making use of the rich cultural diversity within an organisation in order to improve outcomes for individuals, as well as the bottom line of the organisation (Cope & Kalantzis, 1997). This stage is referred to by Hanson (2010) as the 'liberal' model. Recent changes in policy see implementation strategies aimed at increasing the participation rates of students from low socio-economic groups, while at the other end of the spectrum, universities are allowed to offer full cost recovery enrolment pathways to students in selected, high-demand disciplines such as medicine and dentistry. It is the focus on productive diversity that provides a rich medium for the development of students as global citizens.

Global Citizenship: A Contested Term

While the term 'global citizenship' has emerged relatively recently in the literature, it can be argued that the concept has been in existence for over 2,500 years in one form or another. Several commentaries on global citizenship refer to Socrates' timeless claim: 'I am not an Athenian or a Greek, but a citizen of the world.' (Bowden, 2003; Nussbaum, 2002). This statement captures the core concept underlying global citizenship: viewing one's self not only in terms of national identity, but as part of the wider global community.

In relation to tertiary education, global citizenship and the related concept of internationalisation started to emerge as key concepts in the literature from the 1980s (Knight, 2004). However, despite its widespread usage, the term global citizenship remains a contested concept (Bowden, 2003; Ibrahim, 2005; Muetzelfeldt & Smith, 2002; Roman, 2003). Many frameworks for the examination of global citizenship have been proposed, from a broad macro perspective of universal citizenship and human rights (Roche, 2002), to a micro perspective encompassing the knowledge, skills and values required by individuals to thrive in a world characterised by rapid social, cultural and environmental change (Ibrahim, 2005; Tarrant & Sessions, 2008). We argue that both the macro and micro level conceptualisations are important. We favour the conceptualisation of 'globally responsible citizenship' because it recognises the needs of the individual, as well as their responsibilities to society more broadly (Falk, 1993; Roman, 2003). In effect, it recognises the symbiotic nature of the relationship between the self, others and the world (Killick, 2009). Globally responsible citizenship encompasses the need to be aware of and respect important social, cultural, political and economic differences in the world. It also requires individuals to recognise the impact of rapid change on the world's social, cultural and ecological environments, and the need for sustainability in these areas (Barnett, Parry, & Coate, 2001).

What then is the role of higher education in equipping graduates to live, work and make sense of the knowledge and realities that surround them in a world characterised by changeability, uncertainty, turbulence, insecurity and risk (Barnett, 1998)? More specifically, how do we equip the teachers of these graduates who inhabit this same dynamic world? Are academic staff meant to have the answers to the pressing question of how to become a globally responsible citizen? If so, what are the cognitive, affective and behavioural changes that we hope to see in students, and how might teachers catalyse these changes?

In times of turbulence, there is a pressing imperative to hold fast to what is known. In the context of universities, one of these 'knowns' is the relationship between learning and teaching. According to McFarlane (1995, p. 52):

> Learning is an interactive and dynamic process, in which imagination drives action in exploring and interacting with an environment. It requires a dialogue between imagination and experience. Teaching provides the relevant experience and mediates the ensuing dialogue.

In this conception of learning and teaching, a heavy burden of responsibility for imparting 'relevant experience' seems to fall on the shoulders of the one who teaches. It is surprising, therefore, that to date there has been little emphasis on improving the skills and competencies of educators in relation to globally responsible citizenship. This paper aims, through the use of a case study, to provide a possible model for the incorporation of professional development strategies for global citizenship within the university setting.

Academic Development for Global Citizenship – Finding a model

As indicated earlier, policy reforms introduced in Australia in the 1980s brought about a renewed emphasis on the quality of learning and teaching, student outcomes and student satisfaction, and subsequent performance evaluation of academic staff. Increasingly, students' evaluations of courses and their lecturers became the benchmark by which quality of teaching was measured. The importance of ensuring quality in learning and teaching, and various models for examining the scholarship of teaching, are discussed extensively in the literature (Kreber & Cranton, 2000; Trigwell, Martin, Benjamin, & Prosser, 2000). These models, which emphasise the need for staff not only to improve student learning, but also to examine their own teaching practice, led to the inception of professional/academic development programs for academic staff (Lee, Manathunga, & Kandlbinder, 2010). A large research project commissioned by the Australian government found preparation and support for staff in their teaching roles to be uneven and unsystematic, with low enrolments in professional development programs. The research suggested that while there are adequate supports available to academic staff in their research role, "there is no commensurate rigour in the preparation and ongoing support for the teaching role" (Dearn, Fraser, & Ryan, 2002).

Several theoretical models have been put forward for examining professional development in the education sector (Clegg, 2009). One useful conceptualisation of professional development is provided by Land (2001), who identifies 12 distinct orientations for the introduction of academic development. The orientations he identifies are: managerial; political strategist (investor); entrepreneurial; romantic (ecological humanist); vigilant opportunist; researcher; professional competence; reflective practitioner; internal consultant; modeller-broker; interpretive; and discipline specific. In relation to this study, two of the orientations identified by Land are of particular importance. Our case study identifies the university's model as a combination of the 'managerial' and 'entrepreneurial' orientations of professional development. We assert that these predominantly top-down, internally-focused approaches, while having some strengths, are not adequate for professional development in the area of global citizenship. We argue that an alternative strategy, which incorporates elements of the 'reflective practitioner' approach, may be more appropriate. In the reflective practitioner model a bottom-up approach is utilised, in which the client (academic staff member) is central to the learning process. We argue that in order for professional development in the area of internationalisation and 'global citizenship' to be successful, it seems that a combination of top-down and bottom-up approaches is optimal. Further, there is scope for the diffusionist or 'middle-out' model (Caruana & Hanstock, 2008), in which academic staff are central to the development of a 'community of inquiry' related to the topic, and where critical reflection and collaborative inquiry occur with colleagues and with students in the classroom environment.

The Study

The case study is based on an audit (conducted specifically for the purposes of this research study) of how internationalisation is implemented at an urban Australian multi-campus university from the broad strategic to the micro level. Data sources included policies and strategic documents, analysis of communities of practice, curriculum review tools and the integration of graduate attributes in multiple discourses throughout the institution.

Established in the mid 1970s to cater for the rapidly expanding tertiary education sector, the University offers more than 300 degrees across five campuses spanning a 100 kilometre highway. It is home to more than 40,000 students from 124 countries. Classed as one of six Innovative Research Universities, it is among the ten largest higher education providers in Australia. The organisation employs approximately 1200 academic and 2000 administrative staff.

The institutional culture at this university can be categorised as an 'enterprise' culture in which "the knowledge and skills of experts and the needs and wishes of those seeking their services, come together" (McNay, 1995, p. 107). The emphasis on preparing graduates to meet the needs of the market has important implications for the type of professional development strategy utilised. It is argued that the top-down approach to professional development, similar to the managerial and entrepreneurial orientations outlined by Land (2001), does not lead to diffused professional development at the coal face. The managerial orientation is concerned with 'developing staff towards achievement of institutional goals and mission' (Land, 2001, p. 6), while the entrepreneurial orientation aims to foster 'innovative practice related to needs of [the] world of work', but not necessarily the needs of the client (in this case the academic staff). Both of these 'top-down' orientations are sub-optimal in fostering capacity building of staff in the area of global citizenship.

Policies and strategic documents

An audit of policy documents, mission statements, strategic and operational plans indicates a number of important goals in the area of internationalisation. The University has adopted Knight's (2003) definition of internationalisation as: 'the process of integrating an international, intercultural or global dimension into the purpose, functions or delivery of post secondary education' (p. 2). The internationalisation strategy involves recruitment of academic and professional staff from CALD backgrounds, working with international partners in teaching and research, and developing student and staff exchange and study abroad programs. It emphasises that the richness of the university community provides an environment in which all members can share the views and aspirations of others with widely differing experiences, and prepares its members for a role in the global marketplace of ideas, solutions and work (Griffith University Internationalisation Strategy, 2007).

In the area of staff development its goals include:

* Providing staff with the training and skills necessary to teach diverse student groups with different learning styles and traditions;
* Providing training and support for staff to develop an internationalised perspective;
* Encouraging staff to use blended cohorts of Australian and international students as a resource in the learning environment to explore the diversity in their classrooms, to develop a more truly global outlook and identity, and to feel comfortable working with cultural and racial differences;
* Providing professional staff with the training and skills necessary to facilitate positive student experiences for international student clients.

Two other strategic documents crucial to understanding the University's approach to the development of global citizenship are the recently revised 'Graduate Attributes' and the 'Principles to Promote Excellence in Learning and Teaching'. Turning first to the graduate attributes, one of the attributes titled 'Competent in Culturally Diverse and International Environments' has the following sub-attributes:

* Awareness and respect for indigenous knowledge of Aboriginal and Torres Strait Islander peoples;
* Respect, awareness, knowledge and skills to interact effectively in culturally or linguistically diverse contexts;
* A global and international perspective on their disciplines.

These sub-attributes, along with another attribute titled 'Socially Responsible and Engaged in their Communities', comprise the essential characteristics of a global citizen. How these can be incorporated into objectives, content, learning experiences and assessment in the curriculum is the subject of an on-going professional development series.

Linked to the graduate attributes are the Principles to Promote Excellence in Learning and Teaching. Two Principles particularly relevant to the development of global citizenship are:

- Provide learning experiences that develop inter-culturally capable graduates who can make a difference as socially and ethically responsible global citizens;
- Value and recognise individual and cultural diversity through the provision of an inclusive context of support and respect for all students.

While the Principles are the subject of professional development activities, the extent to which they are actually implemented in the classroom is still very much open to question. This is a classic case of a top-down strategy which needs to be complemented by comprehensive approaches to skill development and acquisition (Hess, 2009, p. 456)

Professional Development Activities

The provision of professional development activities in the area of internationalisation is undertaken primarily by the central academic development unit, the human resource management office, and various Communities of Practice across the University. A professional development calendar of activities, a Graduate Certificate in Higher Education, good practice guides and toolkits are offered by the academic development unit of the university. Internationalisation has been the focus of some of these resources and a Good Practice Guide: Internationalising the Curriculum, which recognises the importance of preparing students as global citizens, has been prepared and distributed. Workshops are frequently offered to introduce the Good Practice Guides to staff and to provide exemplars of learning and teaching strategies in the strategic areas of internationalisation and global citizenship. While evaluations are undertaken of these workshops and resources, the results of these are rarely – if ever – viewed by academic or professional staff outside of the central unit.

Incidental learning about internationalisation of the curriculum may take place through staff engagement with embedding graduate attributes in their course profiles, or through use of an annual degree monitoring tool which focuses on the extent of internationalisation in the curriculum, among other things. Once again, the top-down approach does not actively engage academics in self-reflection and diffusion of innovation across the organisation.

Communities of practice

Another avenue for professional development is Communities of Practice (CoP). They offer academics opportunities to work together, over time, on matters of genuine concern within their own contexts in ways that traditional staff development programs cannot (Boud & Middleton, 2003). One CoP at the University is dedicated to cultural diversity and internationalisation. It is a space where professional and academic staff and managers meet to discuss issues around internationalisation and global citizenship, as well as plan seminars, workshops and symposia. These events can be attended from between 35 to (less typically) 400 participants. Approximately 20 staff regularly attend CoP meetings, representing many different disciplines and professional staff elements across the university. Currently on the agenda for discussion is a proposal to introduce a university-wide Global Citizenship program for students and staff. The diverse CoP membership provides an important sounding board for critiquing the proposal before it is put to senior staff in the University.

Young and Mitchell (2003) argue that we need to better understand how CoPs are structured, what makes them 'tick', what institutional factors support or undermine them. While CoPs are mentioned in the University's academic plan, they do not report to any University official committee, and so tend to operate 'under the radar'. Their role in acting as a diffusionist model for change and their impact on learning and teaching quality needs to be evaluated. Wilson and Berne (1999) argue that there needs to be a 'critical colleagueship' in CoPs, where there is a privileging of teachers' interactions with each other, where trust and community can be built while aiming for professional discourse that includes, but does not avoid critique. This is an essential element of professional practice that could be part of continuous peer review.

Learning and teaching grants and awards

A demonstration of the valuing of 'walking the talk' in this University has been an institution-wide grant (valued at $150,000) titled 'Embedding Internationalisation of the Curriculum: A multilevel capacity building process'. Personnel involved with the grant (one of whom has been seconded to the academic development unit) are engaging in professional development activities with staff in several schools across the University. The focus of these activities include student mentoring, group work with students from diverse backgrounds, developing a 'global leaders' program, working on developing graduate attributes to reflect the internationalisation agenda, developing items for course and teaching evaluations, the development of good practice guides, and a program review tool for internationalisation of the curriculum. The latter is being evaluated by international and national members of the project's reference group. As part of the diffusionist approach, wherever possible, 'champions' in the area of internationalisation in different schools have been used as catalysts in curriculum projects.

Discussion and Conclusions

A wide range of perspectives are provided in the literature on why internationalisation and global citizenship are important: however, there is a dearth of research into issues surrounding the conceptualisation of these constructs, and the theoretical and ideological underpinnings on which they are built. Despite this lack of clarity there is general agreement that global citizenship is 'a good thing' and that we should strive to ensure that our students have 'it'. However, there is a lack of research into: (i) the extent to which academics have skills in the area of global citizenship; (ii) how academics should develop their skills in the area; and (iii) whether they desire to develop these skills.

Clearly, it is important to focus on the skills enhancement of our educators in order to ensure that students develop competencies in the area of globally responsible citizenship. It is important not only to consider what types of professional development opportunities are available, but to what extent these are availed of, and how successful they are at achieving their aims of leading to staff development. The evidence suggests that the top-down approach, while useful in bringing global citizenship onto the agenda, does not adequately address how it can be implemented in professional development programs and initiatives. This point is illustrated well through Otten's (2003) comparison between 'intercultural encounters' and 'intercultural competence'. Otten argues that 'intercultural encounters do not automatically increase the intercultural competence of students' (Otten, 2003, p. 15) and that without engaging in an intercultural learning process, students cannot be expected to gain the competencies to interact effectively with people from diverse cultural backgrounds, surely the hallmark of global citizenship. Similarly, we cannot expect staff from a range of disciplines across higher education to know instinctively how to create the type of classroom experiences that encourage students to develop as respectful, socially responsible citizens of the world.

In this chapter we argue that by providing professional development programs in cultural learning and intercultural competency, academic staff can gain the awareness, knowledge and skills to enhance the diversity inherent in the classroom. We have described how the 'top-down' approach to professional development at one university, while successfully bringing internationalisation onto the agenda, does not adequately address the needs of academic staff. Provision of professional development is fragmented and ad hoc, and lack of adequate evaluation of the programs which are in place means that there is a lack of knowledge as to what exactly these programs are achieving: both in terms of staff knowledge, and in terms of how this is translated in teaching practices. Additionally, although the University values good quality teaching and a scholarship of learning and teaching as evidenced in the listing of awards (e.g. faculty citations for excellence in teaching) and the success of applications for prestigious grants around University priorities, it is not clear how academic staff are rewarded for these achievements in terms of career progression. If 'learning and teaching' achievements are to be viewed with the same prestige as 'academic' achievements (e.g. winning of prestigious research grants and publication in top level journals) they need to be rewarded as such.

In order to ensure the greatest level of buy-in from staff, an alternative model, which incorporates both bottom-up and top-down strategies, may prove more successful. In this approach, staff are empowered through critical reflection and collaborative inquiry. In order for professional development for staff in the area of internationalisation to be successful, those who participate need to be actively involved in and believe in what they are learning, and to be prepared to share this learning with student cohorts. It is also important to ensure that programs remain useful over time for different cohorts, and that programs have lasting effects on those who participate, which can then be passed on to others. By incorporating a bottom-up approach to professional development strategies, whereby staff are actively involved in the learning process, it is possible to ensure that staff:

a) are made aware of, and are involved in, the learning process – i.e. they **understand** what they are learning and why it is important;

b) engage with and 'buy in' to the learning process – i.e. they **appreciate** the importance of what they are learning;

c) practise their new competencies – i.e. their **behaviour** is changed as a result of participation in the program.

These professional development strategies encompass learning processes in the 'cognitive', 'affective' and 'behavioural' domains, and thus ensure that participants are engaged in deep learning, which is sustainable over time. It must be noted, however, that in order to assess the impacts of such training on academic staff classroom practices and student outcomes, there is a requirement for systemic and systematic evaluation and feedback processes.

Another important issue which needs to be considered in relation to the introduction of professional development strategies is the receptiveness of academic staff to innovations in the university. Often reactions such as "not another change!", "when do I get a chance to consolidate?" are heard from academic staff trying to keep abreast of a seemingly constant flow of new policies, procedures and practices. There is a need to ensure that the adoption of new policies is made as easy as possible for staff, who are often overburdened with a wide range of teaching and research responsibilities. Wilson and Berne state that teacher learning should not be bound and delivered, but rather activated (1999) and state that a solution to "bridging the chasm between what one's clients – the teachers – want and expect and one's own goals" (is required (Wilson & Berne, 1999). When universities recognise the need to work from the grassroots level, especially in relation to issues which affect staff directly (such as professional development), it may be possible to ensure a greater level of success in improving staff skills and knowledge in the area of internationalisation and global citizenship.

Finally, it is important to acknowledge that professional development in internationalisation is not something that can be imposed in a 'one size fits all' way. Nor can it be assumed that a broad strategic goal to 'internationalise' teaching and learning will actually result in tangible changes in the classroom. Professional development, rather, has to involve meeting with people at grassroots, determining their needs, and designing experiences to meet these needs. In order for professional development to a) meet the actual needs of academic staff, b) be accepted by staff as something worthwhile, and c) lead to observable transformations in teaching, and thus in the learnings of students, it is necessary to engage in meaningful discussion with staff at grassroots levels in the formulation of its design and implementation. Communities of practice are ideal spaces for this to occur.

References

Australian Education International (2010). International student data. Retrieved September 30, 2010, from **http://www.aei.gov.au/AEI/Statistics/StudentEnrolmentAndVisaStatistics/2010/Default.htm**

Barnett, R. (1998). Supercomplexity and the university. *Social Epistemology: A Journal of Knowledge, Culture and Policy,* 12(1), 43–50.

Barnett, R., Parry, G. & Coate, K. (2001). Conceptualising Curriculum Change. *Teaching in Higher Education,* 6, 435–449.

Boud, D. & Middleton, H. (2003). Learning from others at work: Communities of practice and informal learning. *Journal of Workplace Learning,* 15(5), 194.

Bowden, B. (2003). The Perils of Global Citizenship. *Citizenship Studies, 7,* 349–362.

Brownlie, A. (2001). *Citizenship education: The global dimension.* London: Development Education Association.

Bryant, D. (2006). The everyone, everywhere: Global dimensions of citizenship. *A more perfect vision: The future of campus engagement.* Retrieved 17 April, 2009, from **http://www.compact.org/resources/future-of-campus-engagement/the-everyone-everywhere-global-dimensions-of-citizenship/4259/**

Caruana, V. (2007). Internationalisation of Higher Education: Globalisation Discourse, Institutional Strategy and Curriculum Design. In E. O. Doherty (Ed.), *The Fourth Education in a Changing Environment Conference Book.* California: Informing Science Press.

Caruana, V. & Hanstock, J. (2005, September). *Internationalising the curriculum at home or far away? A holistic approach based on inclusivity,* Paper delivered to the Education for Sustainable Development: Graduates as Global Citizens conference, Bournemouth University, UK.

Caruana, V. & Hanstock, J. (2008). Internationalising the Curriculum: From Rhetoric to Reality at the University of Salford. In A. McKenzie & Shiel, C. *The Global University: the role of senior managers.* London: Development Education Association.

Clegg, S. (2009). Histories and institutional change: understanding academic development practices in the global 'north' and 'south'. *International Studies in Sociology of Education, 19*(1), 53–65.

Coates, H. & Krause, K-L. (2005). Investigating ten years of equity policy in Australian higher education. *Journal of Higher Education Policy and Management 27*(1), 35–47.

Cope, B. & Kalantzis (1997). *Productive diversity: a new, Australian model for work and management.* Sydney: Pluto Press.

Dearn, J., Fraser, K. & Ryan, Y. (2002). *Investigation into the Provision of Professional Development for University Teaching in Australia: A Discussion Paper.* Canberra: DEST.

Falk, R. (1993). The Making of Global Citizenship. In J. Brecher, Brown Childs, J. & Cutler, J. (Ed.), *Global visions: Beyond the new world order* (Vol. 1) (pp. 39–50). Boston: South End Press.

Griffith University Internationalisation Strategy (2007), Retrieved September 30, 2010 from **http://www.griffith.edu.au/data/assets/pdf_file/0018/271620/inter nationalisation-strategy.pdf**

Hanson, L. (2010). Global Citizenship, Global Health, and the Internationalization of Curriculum: A Study of Transformative Potential. *Journal of Studies in International Education, 14*(1), 70–88.

Hess, F. M. (2009). Revitalizing Teacher Education by Revisiting Our Assumptions About Teaching. *Journal of Teacher Education, 60*(5), 450–457.

Holden, C. (2000). Learning for Democracy: From World Studies to Global Citizenship. *Theory into Practice, 39*(2), 74–80.

Ibrahim, T. (2005). Global citizenship education: mainstreaming the curriculum? *Cambridge Journal of Education, 35*, 177–194.

Killick, D. (2009, September). *Global citizenship as identification: Locating ourselves-in-the -world.* Paper presented at the Education for Sustainable Development: Graduates as Global Citizens Conference, Bournemouth University.

Knight, J. (2003). Updated definition of Internationalisation. *International Higher Education, 33*, 2–3.

Knight, J. (2004). Internationalization remodeled: Definition, Approaches and Rationales. *Journal of Studies in International Education, 8*(5), 4–31.

Knight, J. (2003). Updated definition of Internationalisation. *International Higher Education, 33*, 2–3.

Kreber, C. & Cranton, P. A. (2000). Exploring the Scholarship of Teaching. *The Journal of Higher Education, 71*(4), 476–495.

Land, R. (2001). Agency, context and change in academic development. *International Journal for Academic Development, 6*(1), 4–20.

Lee, A., Manathunga, C. & Kandlbinder, P. (2010). Shaping a culture: oral histories of academic development in Australian universities. *Higher Education Research & Development, 29*(3), 307–318.

Lynch, K. (2009). Carelessness: A hidden doxa of higher education. *Arts and Humanities in Higher Education, 9*(1), 54–67.

MacFarlane, G. (1995). Future Patterns of Teaching and Learning. In T. Schuller (Ed.), *The Changing University?* (pp. 52–65). Buckingham: SRHE and Open University Press.

McInnis, C. (1995). Less Control and More Vocationalism: The Australian and New Zealand Experience. In T. Schuller (Ed.), *The Changing University?*(pp. 38–51). Buckingham: SRHE and Open University Press

McKenzie, K. & Schweitzer, R. (2001). Who Succeeds at University? Factors predicting academic performance in first year Australian university students. *Higher Education Research & Development, 20*(1), 21–33.

McNay, I. (1995). From the Collegial Academy to Corporate Enterprise: The Changing Culture of Universities. In T. Schuller (Ed.), *The Changing University?* (pp. 105–115). Buckingham: SRHE and Open University Press.

Muetzelfeldt, M. & Smith, G. (2002). Civil Society and Global Governance: The Possibilities for Global Citizenship. *Citizenship Studies, 6*(1), 55–75.

Nussbaum, M. (2002). Education for Citizenship in an Era of Global Connection. *Studies in Philosophy and Education, 21*, 289–303.

Oakman, D. (2002). 'Young Asians in our homes': Colombo plan students and white Australia. *Journal of Australian Studies, 26*(72), 89–98.

Otten, M. (2003). Intercultural Learning and Diversity in Higher Education. *Journal of Studies in International Education, 7*(1), 12–26.

Ramburuth, P., & Welch, C. (2005). Educating the Global Manager. *Journal of Teaching in International Business, 16*(3), 5–27.

Roche, M. (2002). The Olympics and 'Global Citizenship'. *Citizenship Studies, 6*(2), 165–181.

Roman, L. G. (2003). Education and the Contested Meanings of `Global Citizenship'. *Journal of Educational Change, 4*, 269–293.

Schweisfurth, M. (2006). Education for global citizenship: teacher agency and curricular structure in Ontario schools. *Educational Review, 58*(1), 41–50.

Susnowitz, S. (2009). *Transforming Students into Global Change Agents* Retrieved 17 April, 2009, from **http://www.compact.org/resources/future-of-campus-engagement/transforming-students-into-global-change-agents/4262/**

Tarrant, M. A. & Sessions, L. (2008, December). *Promoting global citizenship: Educational travel and study abroad programs in the South Pacific.* Paper presented at the ISANA International Education Association – 19th International Conference, SkyCity Convention Centre, Auckland.

Trigwell, K., Martin, E., Benjamin, J. & Prosser, M. (2000). Scholarship of Teaching: a model. *Higher Education Research & Development, 19*(2), 155–168.

Wilson, S. M. & Berne, J. (1999). Teacher Learning and the Acquisition of Professional Knowledge: An Examination of Research on Contemporary Professional Development. *Review of Research in Education, 24*, 173–209.

Young, S. & Mitchell, J. (2003, April). *Putting More Practice into Communities of Practice.* Paper presented at The Changing Face of VET, 6th Annual Conference of the Australian VET Research Association, Sydney, New South Wales.

Engaging the gatekeepers: Faculty perspectives on developing curriculum for globally responsible citizenship

4

Wendy Green and Patricie Mertova

Abstract

Internationalising the curriculum (IoC) for globally responsible citizenship calls for a profound re-orientation of teaching and learning in universities. While universities worldwide have embraced this challenge at the level of policy, a gap between rhetoric and practice is commonly observed. This paper investigates the gap from the perspective of academics responsible for implementing change 'at the coalface'. Findings from a study conducted at a large Australian research-intensive university, which included interviews with academics in leadership positions within faculties, highlight two interrelated issues which were inhibiting academics otherwise motivated to internationalise curricula. Firstly there was a pervasive sense of uncertainty about the 'correct' or legitimate definition of IoC. Secondly, legitimate leadership and responsibility within the faculties was a concern. Even many of those who were actively engaged with IoC perceived themselves to be 'informal' leaders, operating without clear direction or support from the University. Implications for practice and further research are discussed.

Introduction

Universities have the potential to become key agents of transformation by playing a pivotal role in the production and democratisation of sustainable knowledge societies in our increasingly interconnected world. Making this a reality, however, will require a significant re-orientation of our approach to teaching and learning: from a predominantly transactional model, predicated on inflows of students and funding, to a transformative one which places students 'at the heart of the university, as a source of cultural capital and intentional diversity' (Jones & Brown, 2007, p. 2), and prepares them to act ethically and effectively as globally responsible citizens. While many universities have embraced this challenge at the level of policy (Childres, 2009; Green & Mertova, 2009), there is a commonly observed gap between rhetoric and practice 'at the coalface', in the faculties where teaching and learning occur (Liddicoat, Eisenchlas & Trevaskas, 2003). This chapter investigates this gap from the perspective of academics responsible for implementing curriculum change within one Australian university.

Defining 'Internationalising the Curriculum' for Globally Responsible Citizenship

'Internationalisation of the curriculum' (IoC), as defined by IDP Education Australia in 1995, has become an internationally recognized term for the process of developing 'curriculum which is internationally oriented, aimed at preparing students for performing (professionally, socially) in an international and multicultural context, and designed for domestic students as well as foreign students'. As such, it enacts, at the very least, the values of a 'liberal' framework, with an emphasis on comparative, global perspectives and the ability to communicate across cultures (Hanson, 2010). Within a more 'transformative' approach, however, these two goals support a third – the ability to act responsibly in the face of global inequities (Clifford, 2008).

The concept of 'global citizenship' has been widely taken up by proponents of IoC to signify this third goal of responsible action in the world; as evidenced, for example, by the theme of the 2010 conference at the Centre for International Curriculum Inquiry and Networking: 'Internationalisation of the curriculum for global citizenship: policies, practices and pitfalls'. However, it must be noted that the term is also widely contested. On the one hand, it carries connotations of cultural 'chauvinism' (Haigh & Clifford, 2009); on the other, it can imply responsibility for ensuring equity and social justice for the global community (Roman, 2003). Due to the contested nature of the term 'global citizenship', 'globally responsible citizenship' will be used here instead. In the context of this paper, 'IoC' denotes a transformational approach to education in, and for, a globalising world, with an emphasis on critical thinking for 'critical being' (Barnett, 1997, p. 1). As such, we are referring to a construct (rather than a set of prescribed practices) (Curro & McTaggart, 2003), which has been informed by transformational learning theory (Mezirow, 2003) and critical approaches to pedagogy (Clifford & Joseph, 2005).

Broad agreement regarding the value and purpose of IoC, as it is outlined here and found in university policies in many countries (Childres, 2009; Green & Mertova, 2009), is yet to be followed through in practice. Although the reasons for this gap are complex, and extend far beyond any one university, one reason may be that the concept calls for profound re-orientation of teaching and learning for individuals and institutions alike. Rogers (1995) observed that innovations, which require individuals to change, demand a highly flexible approach on the part of their institutions: one which takes into account the perspectives of those involved. Understanding of how faculty academics, particularly those in a position to exercise leadership in teaching and learning, engage with IoC is therefore vital.

The Gatekeepers of Curriculum Change

Although a common source of complaint within faculties is the dearth of guidelines for what IoC actually means in practice (Liddicoat et al, 2003), top-down management-driven measures to address this issue will be ineffective because they do not take the nature of academic work into account (Birnbaum, 2000). Faculty academics are the 'gatekeepers' or 'harbingers' of curriculum change: 'basic changes in the curriculum do not occur until faculty in their disciplinary and departmental areas are ready to implement them' (Groennings & Wiley (1990) cited in Green & Schoenberg, 2006, p. 4). Differences between disciplines extend far beyond the content taught: they 'go to the heart of teaching, research and student-faculty relationships' (Becher & Trowler, 2001, p. 4). The developmental nature of the task means that academics responsible for teaching in the faculties need to be intellectually engaged with the concept of IoC, and enabled to interpret it within their own disciplines before they can be expected to develop and implement it.

Looking specifically at academics' willingness to engage with IoC, Mestenhauser (1998) attributed faculty academics' 'resistance' to their 'conceptual confusion about what international education means' (p. 4). Further research probing the relationship between conceptualisation and implementation of IoC in the faculties suggests that it is an academic's understanding of teaching, learning and knowledge, rather than IoC per se, that is functionally linked to his/her responses to this agenda. Clifford (2009) found Becher's (1989) categorisation of the disciplines, based on their understandings of teaching, learning and knowledge, useful to understand academics' responses to IoC. The least sophisticated understandings of IoC were associated with what Becher termed the 'hard pure disciplines' (natural sciences and mathematics), where knowledge and ways of teaching and learning are considered to be universal and culturally neutral. From this perspective, then, there is no need to implement IoC. This view was tempered somewhat by those in the 'hard applied disciplines' (such as engineering), while those in the 'soft disciplines' (humanities and social sciences) tended to associate IoC with a more critical pedagogy (Clifford, 2009). Although Clifford's research is based on evidence from one Australian institution, her findings regarding the hard pure disciplines replicate those from earlier studies (e.g. Bond, Qian & Huang, 2003).

In research conducted at another Australian university, Bell (2004) looked at the willingness of academic staff to engage with the IoC agenda in relation to their understanding of teaching and learning more broadly. She found four distinct positions along a 'spectrum of acceptance', which could be mapped onto Ellingboe's (1998) 'Great Divide between attitudes of curricular and systemic change' (Ellingboe, cited in Bell, 2004). On the left of the divide were those with negative attitudes towards change and those who believed IoC to be inappropriate for their discipline: this group ascribed to a content-focused curriculum, and perceived major obstacles to the development of IoC. On the right of divide were those who viewed IoC positively and perceived minimal obstacles to its implementation: this group focused on teaching methodology and learning activities as well as content. Interestingly, Bell's findings resonate with research on academics' conceptions in another, interrelated area of contestation and change – 'graduate attributes' (Barrie, 2004) – which, as Haigh and Clifford (2009) point out, actually provides a framework for IoC development and implementation. All these studies point to a functional link between an academic's understanding and approach to pedagogy and his/her openness to changes in teaching and learning, and suggest that systemic change requires far more than an institutional definition to clarify a particular concept (Green, Hammer & Star, 2009) – although this may be one important step in the right direction.

This study was designed to extend current understandings about differences in academics' approaches to IoC by investigating the perceptions and practices of those in positions of curriculum leadership within the disciplines. The Australian Learning and Teaching Council

(ALTC) has identified the considerable potential of a 'neglected group' of prospective curriculum leaders – for example, Teaching and Learning Deans, Heads of Schools, Chairs of Teaching and Learning Committees – who can 'influence, motivate, and enable others to contribute' at the coalface of teaching and learning (Anderson & Johnson, 2006, p. 2–3). Engaging this 'neglected group' is particularly important in relation to IoC, because the process calls for a comprehensive, developmental approach across degree programmes, rather than courses (or units of study) (Olson, Green & Hill, 2005/2008).

Case Study

Context and methodology

This study was conducted in one large research-intensive Australian university, as part of an institution-wide action research project, headed by the University's Executive. It must be noted, at the outset, that the University has not yet explicitly defined IoC, nor has it developed specific policies, strategies or targets in this area, although it is anticipated that these will be developed in the near future, partially informed by the research reported here. Nevertheless, IoC has been implicitly supported for several years, in other policy documents, such as the University's strategic plan for teaching and learning, and through the implementation of graduate attributes (Green & Mertova, 2009). Like other 'larger, older, research universities', the University under study 'has a number of loosely federated faculties within a highly devolved organisational structure' (Anderson & Johnson, 2006, p. 7). Responsibility for curriculum lies predominantly with the faculties, in this case seven, each of which has several schools, which have generally been formed through the 'clustering' of related disciplines. In addition, many of the University's research institutes' contribution to teaching and learning is supported by a strategic initiative to promote research-rich teaching in all degree programmes.

One of the researchers conducted semi-structured interviews with 115 academics, who held the following positions;

- At the faculty level: Executive Deans; Associate Deans, Academic (ADA); Associate Deans, Research (ADR); and the one Associate Dean, International;
- At the school level: Heads of Schools (HoS); School Teaching and Learning Chairs (TandL Chair);
- Research Institutes: Directors

The interviews, which lasted from ten minutes to one hour, depending on how much the interviewees wanted to say, were recorded, transcribed and analysed. We began the analysis of the data with a list of potential themes drawn from the literature, and our approach was inductive and iterative. As significant themes began to emerge, we structured our analysis accordingly.

In reporting the findings below, pseudonyms are used to ensure anonymity. For the same reason, Becher's (1989) four disciplinary categories, rather than precise disciplinary details are used as follows:

- hard pure (HP) includes the natural sciences and mathematics;
- hard applied (HA) includes science based professions;
- soft pure (SP) includes social sciences/humanities;
- soft applied (SA) includes the social professions, such as education.

Details of individuals' position are provided where relevant to the discussion, but are not linked to their disciplinary groupings.

Findings

Perhaps not surprisingly, given the lack of a clear IoC policy at the time of the study, the interviews with curriculum leaders at all levels and positions across the University revealed a pervasive sense of confusion and uncertainty about the 'correct' institutional definition of IoC. This was regardless of their personal understanding and commitment. Most interviewees began with comments like 'well, I don't know that we have a working definition'. This perceived lack of a 'correct' or 'working' definition needs to be understood within the Australian context. Although there is broad international agreement on the 'liberal' (Hanson, 2010), if not the 'transformative' aims (Clifford, 2008) of IoC, most Australian universities have shaped their own definitions and policies (Green & Mertova, 2009), in ways that reflect their institutional contexts and philosophical orientations. Thus, it is understandable that faculty and school leaders might feel the need for clearer direction and support from the University, regardless of their personal views.

Another relatively unsurprising finding, given findings from other studies (e.g. Bell, 2004; Clifford, 2009), was the wide variation of interest in IoC among those interviewed. At one end of the spectrum were those who did not feel that they had any role to play in internationalising the curriculum. At the faculty level, this group was predominantly made up of the ADRs and Directors of the Institutes.

In spite of the commitment to research-led teaching at this University, the following response from one ADR was typical of this group: 'my responsibility is more to do with research, so with the curriculum my input is minimal.' At the school level, this view was shared by some HoS and TandL Chairs, though at this level, it was usually also associated with a professed lack of understanding about the concept itself. Within this group were many whose limited conceptualisation of curriculum, teaching and learning would place them on the left side of Ellingbone's Great Divide (Bell, 2004); i.e., interpreting 'curriculum' as 'content', they tended to view IoC negatively as something to add to an already 'packed' curriculum.

It must be noted that those interviewed in schools representing the hard pure disciplines generally (though not always) differed from other responses found in the other school interviews, in that they assumed the 'international' or 'universal' nature of their knowledge meant that IoC did not concern them. The phrase 'we think of our discipline/s as essentially universal' was typical of these responses. Although the limited nature of this study cannot support any generalisable conclusions regarding disciplinary variations, it is worth noting that the assumption of universality in the pure science disciplines, and the consequent perception of a lack of relevance of IoC, has been highlighted in previous research (e.g. Clifford, 2009).

Of greater significance to those concerned with processes of curriculum change are the findings relating to those academics who could be characterised as proponents of IoC. This group, consisting of almost all of the ADAs at the faculty level, and a large number of HoS and TandL Chairs at the school level, spoke of two sources of confusion regarding 'legitimacy', which were inhibiting their work in this area. Firstly, in the face of uncertainty about the 'correct' or legitimate institutional definition of IoC, many assumed their own, often reflective and well-informed practices were not supported by, reflected in, or stood at odds with institutional thinking. This confusion or perceived dissonance between personal and institutional definitions was related to a second problem: a question of legitimate leadership and responsibility within the faculties. Even those who were actively engaged with IoC typically perceived themselves to be informal leaders in this area, operating 'under the radar', without clear direction or support from the University.

While a range of institutional factors were seen to inhibit the implementation of IoC, the gap between the willingness to implement IoC and the perceived ability to do so within faculties and schools proved to be one of the most significant and unexpected of our findings. As other perceived inhibitors, such as the need for support to 'concretise' IoC in the disciplines, harness the cultural diversity of staff and students in order to enrich teaching, and address wider student welfare issues, have been reported in detail elsewhere (Green & Mertova, 2009), this gap between willingness and perceived ability will be the focus of our analysis below. For the most part, both the faculty and school groups will be considered together, but significant points of difference will also be highlighted.

Understandings of the concept among proponents of IoC

In spite of the uncertainty about the University's 'correct' or 'formal' definition, those positively disposed towards IoC made it clear that they held strong personal views about its concept and the practice. These personal understandings proved to be informed, comprehensive, and consistent with the literature; they were also surprisingly similar across most faculties, although the interviewees typically referred to examples of practice within their own disciplines to illustrate their ideas. This group of leaders saw IoC as essential and integral: 'it is core curriculum, not just as an optional extra that a few students can engage with if they want to, without embedding it in the courses. It's a central part of every student's experience' (Elizabeth, HA). The only significant difference within this group concerned the portability of qualifications: this was important to those within predominantly 'professional' faculties – although they generally stressed that this was only one aspect of IoC. Otherwise, the 'personal' views of those positively disposed towards IoC in the faculty and school leadership resonated with each other and with the literature; i.e. they saw an internationalised curriculum as having most, or all of the following characteristics:

- **Inclusive**: where the presence of culturally and linguistically diverse students is seen to change the nature of the curriculum, rather than something requiring remediation (e.g. Lawrence, 2003). For example:

We are teaching people from very different backgrounds. Embracing that more, recognising that changes the nature of the course. ... [It isn't] about speaking to any particular cohort of students but making sure that it is accommodating ... (Susan, SP/SA)

- **Comparative and reflexive**: where developing comparative perspectives becomes a way of reflecting on one's own culture, and the cultural construction of one's own knowledge and ways of understanding knowledge. For example:

How do you study philosophy in France, versus how you study it in English speaking countries? ... students [must have] an opportunity to see the way in which the particular approach we take to a subject is itself conditioned culturally (Eric, SP).

- **'Intentionally' diverse**: where diversity means designing for enriched learning for all (e.g. Jones & Brown, 2007), but particularly those who cannot leave home to study abroad. For example:

It's also about ensuring that those international experiences are brought into the curriculum – the core curriculum – so that the students who don't get the opportunity to spend some time abroad actually get exposure ... it's a central part of every student's experience (Elizabeth, HA).

- **Global and local**: where there is a recognition of the dynamic and shifting relationship between the global and the local (Shiel, 2006). As one interviewee said:

[this wouldn't] mean there was no place for local content. For instance, teaching Australian political institutions ... in terms of understanding and appreciating different perspectives on a country's political institutions. The work we've already done on indigenous aspects of the curriculum is also important here (Susan, SP/SA).

* **Interdisciplinary**: where other disciplinary knowledge(s) and ways of thinking contribute to students' developing understanding that 'the fates of nations, individuals and the planet are inextricably linked' (Engberg & Green, 2002, p. 3). For example:

> I hope our students would also acquire, while they're learning here, knowledge about the global issues and how that impacts on [their future practice as professionals] … the global economy and so on (Helene, HA).

* **'Informal'**: where the formal curriculum is designed to promote informal, but meaningful interaction between international and domestic students (Leask, 2009). For example:

> having [students] working together across the boundaries … The curriculum could in fact foster this…. things like peer mentoring, buddy sessions, using video conference sessions. The curriculum makes a good springboard for this (Kathleen, HP).

With their understanding that learning needs to be 'contextual, discursive, experiential, inclusive and critical' (Bell, 2004), these curriculum leaders would clearly be situated on the 'right' side of Ellingboe's 'Great Divide'. Although unable to comment definitively on how they developed this level of understanding, as it was beyond the scope of this study, we can surmise that some have been motivated and supported by their professional accreditation bodies, while others may have initially been inspired by life/work experiences, disciplinary interests, and/or participation in the University's staff development programme for academics.

While those at the faculty and school levels committed to IoC were similarly oriented on the 'right' side of Ellingboe's 'Great Divide', there were some noteworthy differences between these levels. Firstly, among IoC proponents within the schools, there were two common misconceptions: that IoC would be a top-down initiative, requiring a universal curriculum, which would therefore be at odds with disciplinary pedagogies; and that it would preclude the study of local issues, such as Australian Indigenous cultures and other local communities. The perceived mismatch between institutional and disciplinary understandings did not seem to prevent IoC innovation at the school level: in fact, this research project uncovered many examples of IoC, which had been unknown outside (and sometimes inside) the school involved. This work, often driven by single individuals, needs to be understood within the context of research-intensive universities, where 'loosely confederated faculties' particularly prize individual academic autonomy (Anderson & Johnson, 2006). As Gibbs (2005) has noted, pedagogical initiatives in research-intensive universities tend to come from the departments (schools in our case), acting independently of the centre.

Nevertheless, many interviewees said they would like to see more sharing between disciplines. They voiced a sense of operating 'under the radar', without strategic direction, isolated, uncertain about the value or interest of their work outside of their own (sub)disciplinary context, and very much under-appreciated. In this sense, they approximated the 'innovators', rather than the 'early adopters' in Rogers' (1995) categorisation of individual approaches to change; i.e., they were not necessarily integrated into the social system of the organisation, and therefore had limited capacity to act as opinion leaders and change agents. This finding, common in universities (Ramsden, 1998), was exacerbated by the absence of a clear institutional definition, policy and strategies regarding IoC, which in turn contributed to a second issue: perceptions about legitimate leadership.

Proponents' perceptions of responsibility for the carriage of IoC

At the University presented here, curriculum leadership positions have been formalised at the faculty level, but not (yet) at the school level. In the faculties, the role description of the ADAs explicitly includes the requirement to promote the 'internationalisation [of the] Faculty's degree programmes'. Thus, they could be described as inhabiting 'formal' positions of leadership; i.e., they have authority by virtue of their position (Anderson & Johnson, 2006). In contrast, no reference is made to responsibility for IoC in the role description for the HoS; and at the time of the interviews, TandL Chairs had no description of their role written into University policy. The latter operate very much as 'informal' leaders (Anderson & Johnson, 2006), who engage in 'practical and everyday' processes of 'supporting, managing, developing and inspiring academic colleagues' (Ramsden, 1998, p. 4). Regardless of the degree of formality however, most proponents of IoC felt unclear about their responsibility for leading change in this area.

In spite of their formal leadership role, and the depth of their own understanding and commitment, the degree to which the ADAs expressed confidence and a sense of legitimacy as IoC leaders varied considerably. At one end of the spectrum, there were two who saw IoC as integral to their leadership. As Elizabeth said, it is:

> a regular part of curriculum development and review... at all levels: discipline, school and faculty. The description of the role of Associate Dean (Academic) provides a very clear statement by the University that [IoC] are designated as being part of the Associate Deans (Academic) portfolio.

In contrast to this perception of leadership, the interviews with the remaining ADAs conveyed a sense of operating predominantly as 'informal' leaders, without a strong sense of authority, from the 'bottom up' in relation to IoC (Anderson & Johnson, 2006).

Nevertheless, they clearly believed that responsibility for the carriage of IoC within their faculties should lie with them:

> I think the logical way to promote [IoC] would be through working with the [ADA] who has responsibility for the curriculum and teaching…. [We are the ones charged with] dealing with the curriculum structures (Luke).

Like most ADAs, Luke saw the lack of an institutional definition regarding IoC as a major impediment to the development of their leadership in this area:

> I think if I went to the schools and said tell me what you're doing about internationalising your curriculum, I would get a lot of questions about well what do you mean by that? …

Or as another put it:

> [There are] abstract notions of curriculum internationalisation, but people don't understand what that means. …there's no agreed understanding … over in [the DVCI's] office (Eric).

The ADAs felt their potential to lead IoC changes in the faculties was further hampered by communication gaps between those above and below them, and between the Offices of senior University executives with responsibility for academic matters. Although some of the ADAs welcomed the 'strategic talk sessions' they had had with the senior Executive regarding other curriculum matters, they felt that more engagement across all levels of leadership was needed regarding IoC. For example:

> where we fall down is in [this communication] gap … it would be good … to work more closely to establish processes or get feedback [We need] strategic talk

> sessions…There's no point just meeting to [hear about]
> formal policy. What would be good would be to discuss
> things more broadly (Brian).

This uncertainty about responsibility for IoC, and poor communication between differing levels of leadership was fundamentally the same, although magnified, at the school level.

Implications

Previous research has indicated that 'resistance' to implementation of IoC is the result of 'conceptual confusion' about IoC (Mestenhauser, 1998), which in turn, is linked to ways of understanding of teaching, learning and knowledge (Clifford, 2009; Bell, 2004). However, this study has shown that the sophisticated pedagogical understanding and willingness to implement IoC found within the 'neglected group' of potential curriculum leaders in the faculties is not sufficient to produce systemic change. For this group, the primary focus of the discussion here, two issues relating to 'legitimacy' within the institution were found to be major inhibiting factors in relation to IoC. Firstly, there was a pervasive sense of uncertainty about the 'correct' or legitimate institutional definition of IoC. Secondly, perceptions of legitimate leadership and responsibility within the faculties were a concern: even those who were actively engaged with IoC generally perceived themselves to be 'informal' leaders, without clear direction or support from the University.

In relation to the first finding, this study concurs with others, which point to the danger of not addressing the need for clear institutional direction. In the US context, Olson and colleagues (2005/2008) found that many institutions have articulated the desire to produce globally-competent graduates, without defining what this means, or a strategy for achievement. The result is that individual academics focus on input – doing more of what they already do, more study abroad, more international examples in course content, etc – without the ability or confidence to make the necessary connection to desired outcomes at the programme level. These findings suggest that direction from the 'top-down' must be clear, but not overly prescriptive, and complemented by bottom-up, disciplinary measures led by those perceived by their colleagues and superiors to be curriculum leaders. The definition adopted by a university should avoid common misconceptions, such as those found here, and focus on the goal (of developing 'globally responsible citizenship'). Yet, for innovation to be effectively implemented, an institutional definition must be developed, not simply handed down from above; there needs to be a shared understanding of IoC across the institution. Rogers describes this process as one of social construction:

> When a new idea is first implemented in an organisation, it has little meaning to the organisation's members … Through a process of the people in the organisation talking about the innovation they gradually gain a common understanding of it. Thus the meaning of the innovation is constructed over time through a social process of human interaction (Rogers, 1995, p. 399).

Such an approach, akin to Laurillard's (1997) 'learning conversations', would meet the needs expressed explicitly by one of the ADAs: not to be told about formal policy, but to be engaged in making it, through 'strategic talk sessions'.

Secondly, this case study underscores the need, identified by the Australian Learning and Teaching Council (ALTC), to support and build the capability of leaders and potential leaders in faculties and schools. The finding of extensive reliance on 'informal' leadership in this study must be seen within the context of traditional approaches to management in universities. Although leadership in universities has traditionally been associated with the most senior academic staff

(D'Agostino & O'Brien, 2009), it is the disciplinary academics who are the 'gatekeepers' of curriculum change, particularly those who hold positions of informal leadership – the programme convenors, and/or those who represent the school's interests on teaching and learning committees. Such positions often come without any line management authority, and without explicit guidelines regarding leadership responsibility. Any attempt to enhance leadership capability would need to address this issue, by either establishing clear role descriptions, or explicitly addressing the challenges posed by informal leadership (Flavell, Jones & Ladyshewsky, 2008). Just as importantly, such an initiative would need to address the perceptions, common across the sector, regarding 'leadership'. The reticence of those, even in formal positions of leadership, to identify as curriculum leaders in this case study is a common finding in universities (Ramsden, 1998). Confusing leadership with management, many academics view it as an alien concept, which undercuts traditional values of 'collegiality, autonomy and freedom based on individual achievement' (Flavell et al, 2008, p. 26). Moves to develop distributed leadership in academe must address the tensions between the traditional values of academic culture, emerging management practices and increased accountability for the quality of student learning. One approach to staff development, developed by Flavell and colleagues (2008) addresses all of these issues – poor role descriptions, the autonomy and disciplinary differences between schools and faculties, the need for academics to be intellectually engaged in change processes, and the enduring emphasis on collegiality – in a programme that includes a focus on 'inter-personal, change management and communication skills' (p. 25). Most notably however, the hallmark of the programme appears to be the time allowed for 'critique, debate and discussion' (p. 27). Such an approach, which engages potential curriculum leaders intellectually with ideas of leadership, as well as developing skills, could be adopted for the purpose of fostering leadership for IoC.

Conclusions

This paper has presented and discussed the findings of a research study concerning academics' perceptions and practices of IoC among a 'neglected group' of curriculum leaders in a large Australian research-intensive university. These findings have implications for addressing the oft-noted gap between rhetoric and practice in relation to IoC for globally responsible citizenship – an undertaking which calls for profound changes to the conceptualisation and practice of teaching and learning in universities. Firstly, this study suggests that a deep understanding and a willingness to implement IoC is not in itself sufficient to produce systemic change. Two interrelated factors were seen to inhibit academics otherwise motivated to internationalise curricula. Firstly, there was a pervasive sense of uncertainty about the 'correct' or legitimate definition of IoC. Secondly, legitimate leadership and responsibility within the faculties was a concern: even most of those who were actively engaged with IoC perceived themselves to be operating in isolation, without clear direction or support from the University. These findings suggest that the emerging literature on organisational change and curriculum leadership in universities has much to offer those committed to fostering globally-minded citizenship through teaching and learning.

References

Anderson, D. & Johnson, R. (2006). *Ideas of leadership underpinning proposals for the Carrick Institute: a review of proposals for the Leadership for Excellence in Teaching and Learning Program*. (Occasional paper). Retrieved December 12, 2009 from **http://www.altc.edu.au/system/files/documents/grants_leadership _occasionalpaper_andersonandjohnson_nov06.pdf**

Barnett, R. (1997). *Higher education: A critical business*. Buckingham, UK: Society for Research into Higher Education and Open University Press.

Barrie, S. (2004). A research-based approach to generic graduate attributes policy. *Higher Education Research and Development, 23*(3), 261–275.

Becher, T. (1989). *Academic tribes and territories: Intellectual enquiry and the cultures of the disciplines.* Milton Keynes, UK: Society for Research into Higher Education and the Open University Press.

Becher, T. & Trowler, P. (2001). *Academic tribes and territories: Intellectual enquiry and the cultures of the disciplines.* (2nd ed.). Buckingham, UK: Society for Research into Higher Education and the Open University Press.

Bell, M. (2004, July). *Internationalising the higher education curriculum: Do academics agree?* Proceedings of the 27th Higher Education Research & Development Society of Australasia (HERDSA) Conference, Miri, Sarawak. Retrieved October 28, 2010 from: **http://www.herdsa.org.au /wp-content/uploads/conference/2004/PDF/P036-jt.pdf.**

Birnbaum, R. (2000). *Management fads in higher education.* San Francisco, C.A: Jossey-Bass.

Bond, S., Qian, J. & Huang, J. (2003). *Role of faculty in internationalizing the undergraduate curriculum and classroom experience.* Ottawa, Canada: Canadian Bureau for International Education.

Childres, L. (2009). Internationalization plans for higher education institutions. *Journal of Studies in International Education, 13*(3), 289–309.

Clifford, V. (2009). Engaging the disciplines in internationalising the curriculum. *International Journal for Academic Development, 14*(2), 133–143.

Clifford, V. (2008). *Internationalising the curriculum resource kit.* Centre for International Curriculum Inquiry and Networking. Retrieved October 28, 2010 from: **http://www.brookes.ac.uk/services/ocsld/ioc/resourcekit.html/**

Clifford, V & Joseph, C. (2005). *Internationalisation of the curriculum: an investigation of the pedagogical practices at Monash University.* Report. Melbourne, Australia: Higher Education Development Unit, Monash University.

Curro, G. & McTaggert, R. (2003, October). *Supporting the pedagogy of internationalisation*. Paper presented at the 17th IDP Australian Education Conference. Melbourne, Australia.

D'Agostino, F. & O'Brien, M. (2009). *Closing the gap in curriculum development leadership: Final report*. Retrieved April 24, 2010 from **http://www.altc.edu.au/system/files/resources/LE605_UQ_D%27A gostino_final_report_March%2010.pdf**

Ellingboe, B. (1998). Divisional strategies to internationalise a campus portrait. In J.A. Mestenhasuer and B. J. Ellingboe (Eds.) *Reforming the higher education curriculum: Internationalizing the campus* (pp. 198–228). Phoenix: Oryx Press.

Engberg, D. & Green, M. (2002). *Promising practices: Spotlighting excellence in comprehensive internationalisation*. Washington DC: American Council of Education.

Flavell, H., Jones, S. & Ladyshewsky, R. (2008, October). Academic leadership development for course coordinators and the influences of higher educational change. *Proceedings of the Australian Universities Quality Forum 2008*, Canberra, Australia. Retrieved February 27, 2010, from: **http://www.auqa.edu.au/ qualityenhancement/publications/occasional/publications/**

Gibbs, G. (2005, July). Being strategic about improving teaching and learning in research-intensive environments. *Proceedings from the International Conference of Higher Education Research & Development Society of Australasia (HERDSA)*. Sydney Australia.

Green, W. & Mertova, P. (2009). *Internationalisation of teaching and learning at The University of Queensland: Perceptions and practices*. Retrieved April 4, 2010 from: http://www.tedi.uq.edu.au/internationalisation/

Green, W., Hammer, S. & Star, C. (2009). Facing up to the challenge: why is it so hard to develop graduate attributes? *Higher Education Research and Development, 28*(1), 17–29.

Green, M.F. & Shoenberg, R. (2006). *Where faculty live: Internationalizing the disciplines*. Washington DC: American Council of Education.

Groennings, S. & Wiley, D. (Eds.) (1990). *Group portrait: internationalizing the disciplines.* New York: The American Forum for Global Education.

Haigh, M. & Clifford, V. (2009, June). Widening the graduate attributes debate: A higher education for global citizenship. In , *Internationalising the home student: Trigger paper for the Centre for International Curriculum Inquiry and Networking Conference,* June, Oxford Brookes University, Oxford, UK.

Hanson, L. (2010). Global Citizenship, Global Health, and the Internationalization of Curriculum: A Study of Transformative Potential. *Journal of Studies in International Education, 14*(1), 70–88.

IDP Education Australia (1995). *Curriculum Development for Internationalisation: Australian Case Studies and Stocktake.* Canberra, Australia: DEETYA.

Jones, E. & Brown, S. (2007). *Internationalising higher education.* London and New York: Routledge.

Laurillard, D. (1997). *Applying systems thinking to higher education.* Position paper, Milton Keynes: Open University.

Lawrence, J. (2003). The deficit-discourse shift: university teachers and their role in helping first year students persevere and succeed in the new university culture, Retrieved April 28, 2005 from: **http://ultibase.rmit.edu.au/Articles/march03/lawrence1.htm.**

Leask, B. (2009). Using formal and informal curricula to improve interactions between home and international students. *Journal of Studies in International Education, 13*(2), 205–221.

Liddicoat, A., Eisenchlas, S. & Trevaskas, S. (2003). *Australian perspectives on internationalising education,* Melbourne: Australia.

Mestenhauser, J.A. (1998). Portraits of an international curriculum: An uncommon multidimensional perspective (pp. 3–39). In J.A. Mestenhasuer & B. J. Ellingboe (Eds.) *Reforming the higher education curriculum: Internationalizing the campus.* Phoenix: Oryx Press.

Mezirow, J. (2003). Transformative Learning as Discourse. *Journal of Transformative Education, 1*(1), 58–63.

Olson, C.L., Green, M.F. & Hill, B.A. (2005/2008). *Building a strategic framework for comprehensive internationalization.* Washington DC: American Council of Education.

Ramsden, P. (1998). *Learning to lead in higher education.* London: Routledge.

Rogers, E.M. (1995). *Diffusion of innovations.* 4th Edition. New York: The Free Press, Simon & Schuster.

Roman, L. G. (2003). Education and the Contested Meanings of `Global Citizenship'. *Journal of Educational Change, 4,* 269–293.

Shiel, C. (2006). Developing the global citizen. *Academy Exchange, 6,* 18–20.

Graduate attributes and education for responsible global citizenship

5

Valerie Clifford and Martin Haigh

Abstract

Publishing a formal statement of Graduate Attributes became a requirement of government funding in Australian universities in 1992; the idea is slowly trickling into UK universities and has yet to reach most of India. However, many university websites now showcase more or less overt statements of the attributes that their graduates will achieve through their studies at the university. Here, we use Wilber's (2006; 2001; Haigh & Clifford, 2011) AQAL (All Quadrants, All Levels) integral analytical technique to explore the fundamental character of the Graduate Attributes in some Indian, Australian and UK universities and ask if these truly reflect the qualities that we need for our future global citizens. This analysis shows that, while all of the universities have a strong commitment to preparing graduates for the workforce, often as professionals and leaders, there is also a focus on a graduate's future place in their local, national and global societies that sometimes includes explicit commitment to the relief of social injustice. However, despite much rhetoric about personal awareness, ethical and moral responsibility, there is less emphasis in the four Western universities than in the two Indian universities, on the development of Individual Interior qualities of personal responsibility. To provide an education for socially responsible active 'global citizenship', Western education will need to give more attention to the development of the personal ethical systems of learners.

Introduction

This chapter explores the conflicting agendas that compete for attention in current attempts to determine the qualities and capabilities of university graduates: the academic, the corporate, and the employer (Twitchell, 2004; Hager & Holland, 2006). It analyses the formal statements made by six universities about the qualities and capabilities that they expect to imbue in their graduates. Undoubtedly, in many cases, these statements are formulaic, but their proliferation is fueling a revival of the age-old debate about what a university education is actually supposed to achieve. Is it about preparing students for employment, creating intellectuals, or developing global citizens (Haigh, 2005; Haigh & Clifford, 2010)? Is the university graduate someone who is well versed in the ways of the past, or someone who creates new ways for the future? There is much talk about the latter but very few universities teach Future Studies as a real discipline (Marien, 2002; Milojevic 2005). Again, if this education is to produce graduates who are either future-proofed or able to produce a better future, what will they need to know and be able to do (Popovic et al. 2010)? Is the answer in ICT or biological technology, education for sustainability and environmental security, critical thinking, reflective practice, autonomous learning, self-awareness or ethics: or does it involve the creation of a new set of values to replace the individualism and materialism of our present society; something involving, perhaps spirituality or religion (Inayatullah, 2010; McKenzie et al., 2008)?

Previously, we set out (and later analysed) our view of what graduate attributes should be developed by a university education (Haigh & Clifford, 2010; 2011). Barrie (2006) suggests that academics tend to view graduate attributes from four different perspectives, which we paraphrase as Table 1.

Perspective	Graduate Attribute Development
Precursor conception	Students arrive at University with generic graduate attributes – all the university needs to do is add disciplinary knowledge.
Complement conception	Graduate attributes are qualities that emerge as an inevitable outcome of a discipline-based education.
Translation conception	Graduate attributes emerge from those discipline-specific skills that abet the constructive and creative application of disciplinary knowledge to new contexts. These skills include qualities such as emotional intelligence and critical awareness.
Enabling conception	Graduate attributes are the qualities of an 'educated person' and so represent a sophisticated level of intellectual, personal and moral development. An educated person is respected as much for their general knowledgeability as for any particular disciplinary expertise, and for their capacity to create, collate and apply knowledge appropriately to new circumstances.

Table 1. Four Academic Perspective on Graduate Attributes (after Barrie, 2006)

Barrie covers the spectrum of arguments from those that suggest that worrying about graduate attributes is a waste of time to those that argue that their development is the most important role of education. Our position is closer to Barrie's fourth 'Enabling Conception', which sees graduate attributes in whole person terms, but with a stronger emphasis on global citizenship and moral cosmopolitanism (Hill, 2000). In our work we sought the essence of what we might wish of our graduates.

Our initial view was that we should address two key concerns: first, we should educate graduates who are good citizens, the kind of responsible and ethical people we would wish to have as neighbours and leaders of our communities; and second, we felt that we should educate people who would be able to earn their own living and fend for themselves in a self-sustaining world. We expressed the result in two tables, the first containing citizenship attributes (responsible, capable, compassionate, self-aware, ecoliterate, cosmopolitan and employed) (Table 2).

Graduate Attributes	Associated Abilities and Skills
Responsible Citizens	Graduates are aware of their personal responsibilities to the future wellbeing of society and environment – most especially to the welfare of future generations.
Capable Citizens	Graduates are able to do as well as to know. They have skills in problem solving, communication, and leadership – that can be applied broadly.
Compassionate Citizens	Graduates demonstrate a capacity of empathy for others and treat all of their interactions with sensitivity, compassion and a concern for social justice.
Self-aware Citizens	Graduates are reflective practitioners who understand their own personal attributes, capabilities, weaknesses, strengths, limitations goals and priorities.
Ecoliterate Citizens	Since sustainability is the greatest challenge facing human society, graduates offer informed leadership and set a good personal example.
Cosmopolitan Citizens	Graduates should be capable of functioning effectively, flexibly and constructively in an inter-cultural/global environment. They are socially responsible and sensitive to other people's cultures and belief systems.
Employed Citizens	Graduates are capable of earning a living because they are equipped with the skills and attributes that society needs.

Table 2. Citizenship Attributes – the arts of living in harmony (Abbreviated from Haigh & Clifford, 2010).

Our second table contained attributes relating more directly to employability (Haigh and Clifford, 2010; 2011). However, as Harvey (2005, p. 13) states, '... employability is not just about getting a job; it is about developing attributes, techniques, or experience for life. It is about learning, and the emphasis is ... more on "ability." ... developing critical reflective abilities, with a view to empowering and enhancing the learner. Employment is a by-product of this enabling process'. Nevertheless, our very production of two tables demonstrates our uncomfortable recognition of two competing ethics in the path of our graduates 'learning to know' (Delors, 1996). The first, the ethic of education for global citizenship, concerns justice, social responsibility and environmental sustainability, in sum – the ethics of 'learning to be' and 'learning to live together' (Delors, 1996). The second ethic emphasises 'learning to do', but the employability goals of competitive advancement of individual careers, of being entrepreneurial, and getting good jobs to boost the national economy, often seem to contradict those stated earlier (Delors, 1996).

Integral Analysis

In an attempt to construct a clearer perspective on the problem, we adopted an approach based on the Integral Analysis of Ken Wilber, better known as AQAL (All Quadrants, All Levels, Lines, States and Types) (Haigh & Clifford, 2011; Wilber, 2006; 2001). Wilber argues that as a first step to understanding a social situation completely, one should consider it from at least four viewpoints. These are the points of view of the individual and the collective, which is the perspective that informed our two tables above, and two further perspectives – the view from the inside (interior) and that from the outside (exterior) (Table 3 overleaf).

When we mapped our own proposals for Graduate Attributes, we found that almost all of the attributes in Table 1 mapped into the lower left quadrant, the social interior. Most of our Employability table was expressed in the language of the individual exterior, although it did try and suggest the development of some whole-person qualities (cf. Harvey, 2005). Of course, the capacity of an individual to gain and retain 'fulfilling work' may also be explored at institutional (i.e. collective exterior) levels, for example by means of institutional league tables and quality assurance measures (Harvey, 2001). However, our

	Interior	Exterior
	Pronoun: I	Pronoun S/He or It
Individual	Interior Individual Personal (I – seen from the inside) These are the thoughts and beliefs, feelings, emotions and values of the individual self, which are manifested as intentional behaviours and ambitions. This is the realm of 'what I should be doing' and personal ethics	Individual Exterior (You seen from the outside) This is what I experience of another as expressed through their words, actions, behaviour, attitudes etc. This is the viewpoint of the biographer, objective scientist, colleague or employer.
	Pronoun: We / Us	Pronoun: Them / Its
Collective	Interior Social (Us – seen from the inside) Our expectation of what is expected of members of a society; our acquiescence to values and culture of the collective. This is the realm of duty, culture, responsibility, rights, citizenship and of what ought to be done for and with others.	Exterior Social (You seen from the outside) These are attributes and values that we, as a group, expect or observe in another group. This is the viewpoint of the social scientist or anthropologist, the planner or civil servant, and of the statistical analyst. It concerns systems, structures, institutions, and cultural traditions as viewed by an outsider.

Table 3. AQAL Quadrants

conclusion was that more work on the individual interior, the development of personal integrity, was needed to produce citizens who were both responsible and employable (Haigh & Clifford, 2011). The question then arose: to what extent is our experience reflected in Graduate Attribute statements made elsewhere?

This chapter proceeds by analysing six further graduate attribute statements, two from the United Kingdom (Strathclyde and Oxford Brookes Universities), two from Australia (Melbourne and Wollongong Universities) and, by way of contrast, from two rather special universities in India with a radically different Non-Western, post-colonial perspective (Visva-Bharati and Teerthankar Mahaveer Universities). Our analysis continues to consider, question and evaluate the priorities of current higher education. Our key question remains: will such graduate attribute statements contribute to the production of the responsible global citizens that securing the future of our world demands?

Of course, there are huge differences in these three contexts. Higher Education in India is in a phase of explosive growth with plans to increase its student enrolment from about 13 millions today to over 20 millions in the immediate future, a process that will involve the creation of hundreds of new universities, many of them new private institutions. By contrast Higher Education in the UK and Australia may have passed its peak enrolments. All three systems have, historically, been developed by the State but, in a context of diminishing government support are now engaging more with entrepreneurial and marketing endeavour (Haigh, 2008). The two Indian Universities merit special interest, not just because they come from different Non-Western value systems, but because both have preset, rather than corporately negotiated, value systems that were prescribed at their foundation. These are the Hindu, spiritual and arts-humanitarian vision of that pioneer of global citizenship education, Rabindranath Tagore, in the case of Visva-Bharati University (Tagore, 2008); and the ancient ethical code of the Jain religion in the case of Teerthankar Mahaveer University (Jain 'Sadak', 2005). By contrast, the four Western Universities are firmly secular. The University of Melbourne is an elite, world ranked university, while the University of Wollongong, ranked in the better half of Australia's Universities, is distinguished by having strong links with industry (AEN, 2011). The two UK universities are both middle-ranked, although Oxford Brookes University is a leader of the UK's 'Modern (Post-1992) Universities'. Nevertheless, AQAL analysis of this very diverse group of six universities shows that, despite these essential differences, they share many similar concerns.

University of Strathclyde, Glasgow

Our first example is Scotland's University of Strathclyde (n.d.). Here, a research project involving 20 Scottish Higher Education Institutions produced clear awareness of the problem of the two paradigms encountered by our research (QAA (Scotland), 2007). A news release at the time stated that: 'This means looking at the values that inform the work of universities, their contribution to culture, citizenship and intellectual growth, and their ability to educate graduates with the skills they'll need for the world of work' (University of Strathclyde, 2010). However, Strathclyde's objectives are very focussed on enhancing employability (Woolmer, 2009). Their list of attributes address personal qualities and they are expressed in the language of 'being', 'what it means to be a Strathclyde student and become a Strathclyde graduate'. However, the list emphasises operational, employment-related, skills, and hence there are many crucial gaps; not least in the matter of ethics and social concern, which are ignored by this individualist focus. Nevertheless, their six attributes do pay some attention to the individual interior quadrant (Table 4).

	Interior	Exterior
	Interior Individual / Personal	Individual Exterior
Individual	Ethical, identifying risks and taking responsibility	Enquiring, pursuing critical questions Capable, applying leading edge knowledge Creative, contributing to solutions Enterprising, creating opportunities
Collective	Interior Social	Exterior Social
	Global, thinking internationally	Global, in outlook

Table 4. AQAL Analysis of University of Strathclyde Graduate Attributes

Oxford Brookes University, England

	Interior	Exterior
	Interior Individual / Personal	**Individual Exterior**
Individual	Critical self awareness and personal literacy. Understanding how one learns and to identify one's own strength and weaknesses. Independent Thinking. Ability to perform as autonomous, effective and independent learner.	Academic and professional literacy. Disciplinary and professional knowledge and skills, understanding the epistemology and 'landscape' of the discipline Research literacy. Critical consumer of research and ability to undertake a small research project. Digital literacy Good social skills. Ability to relate to others, develop appropriate interpersonal skills, emotional intelligence and adaptive expertise.
	Interior Social	**Exterior Social**
Collective	Good professional citizen. Thinks and behave as a member of that disciplinary/professional community of practice. Global citizenship. Knowledge and skills, showing cross-cultural awareness, and valuing human diversity. How discipline knowledge is represented and understood within other cultures. Confidence to question one's own values and those of others responsibly and ethically; and responsible citizenship, actively engaging with issues of equity, social justice, sustainability and the reduction of prejudice, stereotyping and discrimination	Global citizenship. Working effectively and responsibly in a global context.

Table 5. AQAL Analysis of Oxford Brookes University's Graduate Attributes

Oxford Brookes University has recently developed a 'Strategy for Enhancing the Student Experience 2010–2015' (Oxford Brookes University, 2010a). This lists five graduate attributes, which we unpack as Table 5. Again, we see a focus on the gaining of employability skills but also a wider spread of attributes, with a second focus on developing awareness of self and personal autonomy as well as an awareness of oneself as globally connected and having social responsibilities. However, how that social responsibility will specifically manifest itself is unclear.

The University of Melbourne, Australia

In 2008, the University of Melbourne, one of Australia's leading universities, announced the 'Melbourne Model' (University of Melbourne, 2008) which introduced a more liberal approach to undergraduate studies. This aimed to give learners a breadth of knowledge and the opportunity to pursue new options that opened up during their studies, and is proclaimed as an excellent foundation for moving on to employment or graduate study. These ideas are reflected in their graduate attributes, where personal awareness sits alongside a strong sense of obligation to be a leader, change agent and mentor in their communities (University of Melbourne, 2007). However, the Collective Exterior quadrant is relatively empty; and equally, there is little emphasis on cultivating personal self-development – only self-awareness – in the Individual Interior quadrant (Table 6).

The University of Wollongong, Australia

The University of Wollongong reviewed its graduate qualities in 2006–7 (University of Wollongong, 2010), streamlining three previous sets of attributes. Again there is a strong focus on employment related qualities with a recognition that graduates will operate in local, national, global and professional communities. Although, in many

	Interior	Exterior
	Interior Individual / Personal	**Individual Exterior**
Individual	**Self-awareness** of personal strengths and limitations	**Academically excellent** including, knowledge, research skills, problem solving, communication, intellectual integrity, critical and creative thinking. **Knowledgeable across disciplines** including ability to critique, synthesise and evaluate, and for skills to be transferable.
	Interior Social	**Exterior Social**
Collective	**Leaders in communities,** profoundly aware of community needs, a change agent and mentor of others. **Active global citizens,** accepting social and civic responsibilities, being an advocate for environmental sustainability, with a high regard for human rights, equity and ethics. **A well informed citizen,** contributing to communities in which they live and work, understanding and respecting social and cultural diversity.	**Active global citizens and leaders,** advocate for environmental sustainability

Table 6. AQAL Analysis of the University of Melbourne's Graduate Attributes

universities, the institutional graduate attributes will be built upon by faculties and disciplines to illustrate how they relate to the different areas, here, the right of faculties and disciplines to 'interpret' the graduate qualities is written into the document. Wollongong urges each discipline to interpret the qualities into their own language so that they make sense to their students.

	Interior	Exterior
	Interior Individual / Personal	Individual Exterior
Individual	Independent learner. Includes research, enquiry, reflection, critical analysis and evaluation	Informed. Includes knowing, understanding and Capable. Application locally and internationally Problem solvers. Includes creative, logical and critical thinking and decision making. Effective communicators. Includes work collaboratively and recognise how culture can shape communication
	Interior Social	Exterior Social
Collective	Responsible. Understand how decisions can affect others and make ethically informed choices. Appreciate and respect diversity. Act with integrity as part of local, national, global and professional communities	

Table 7 AQAL Analysis of the University of Wollongong's Graduate Qualities

Interestingly, the University of Wollongong in Dubai (n.d.) has an almost identical set of graduate qualities to the Australian campus. There are two differences. The first is in the initial wording where Dubai will 'aim to instill the following qualities in all graduates' while Australia remains 'committed to developing graduates who are'. The second involves the removal, from the Dubai list, of the sixth attribute: 'a flexible approach for faculties'. This raises all kinds of questions about the character and role of international universities and their satellite campuses as well as about the implications of different cultural, educational, social and political contexts for the conceptualisation of graduate attributes.

Our analysis of the home campus attributes finds a familiar emphasis on individual exterior attributes with an admixture of social interior qualities. Despite being an international university, there is no emphasis on the global role of its learners and little about the development of their interior ethical qualities (Table 7).

Visva-Bharati University, Santiniketan, West Bengal, India

Visva-Bharati University is one of India's elite, Government-controlled, Central Universities and one created as 'an institution of

	Interior	Exterior
	Interior Individual / Personal	Individual Exterior
Individual	Self-developing: 'The mantra in our hearts is: "Satyātma, Prānārāmam, Mana Ānandam". That is: "Solace to the Soul, Verity of self, Thou art to me, The joy of my heart"'	Committed to Social Justice: 'One is the emphasis on service to the poor, the downtrodden and the deprived'. Aesthetically Educated 'Another is the joyful integration of music, fine arts, festivals and fairs into the learning process'.
	Interior Social	Exterior Social
Collective	Community Service: 'Dedicated to the service of humanity and the enlightenment of young minds' Socially Integrative: To initiate a dialogue between academic study and research of rural economy / culture and on-field experience. Global Citizenship: To seek to realize in a common fellowship of study the meeting of the East and the West, and thus ultimately to strengthen the fundamental conditions of world peace	International and Cosmopolitan: 'Meeting place of the languages and cultures of India, a repository of Eastern learning, and a dynamic centre of India's understanding and absorption of the West's sciences and culture. It is still very much an international place where students, scholars, intellectuals, pilgrims and tourists from East and West and from all over India gather and mingle...'

All quotes from Ray (2010)

Table 8. AQAL Analysis of Visva-Bharati University's Graduate Qualities

national importance' by its 1951 foundational Act of Parliament. Even today, this University has the President of India as its Paridarsaka (Visitor) and it is the President who appoints the Acharya (Chancellor) and Upacharya (Vice-chancellor). The University claims two Nobel Laureates, Amartya Sen and its founder, Rabindranath Tagore, who began this institution as an educational experiment and who, coincidentally, was a pioneer of the notion of global citizenship education (Tagore, 2008). The university retains an aspiration of Tagore's as its motto: "Yatra visvam bhavatyekanidam", which translates as: "Where the world makes a home in a single nest".

Visva-Bharati University is based on Hindu ideals emphasising the social values of enlightening young minds and serving humanity (Ray, 2010). The university is also dedicated to the uplift of weaker sections of society, especially the cause of rural villagers and tribal (Adivasis) peoples (Visva-Bharati University, 2006) .

AQAL analysis of Visva-Bharati's ambitions for its graduates displays very sharp differences with those of the four Western Universities (Table 8). First, there is very strong self-awareness of its place and role in India and the wider world. Second, there is much deeper concern for the holistic personal development of the learner's person, while the characteristic list of Individual Exterior employment skills is supplanted by the aims of a general education. Clearly Visva-Bharati sees itself as producing an intellectual elite of international significance.

Teerthanker Mahaveer University (TMU), Mordabad, Uttar Pradesh

Teerthanker Mahaveer University (TMU), founded 2008, is a gleaming new private institution founded by India's minority Jain community and as such represents the new wave in India's Higher Education (Agarwal, 2009). Its strap branding line of "An ultimate destination for world class education" signals its aspiration to become India's top private University by providing, mainly, education for the professions, albeit with a commitment to interdisciplinarity (TMU, 2010). The statements of the TMU's aims and the comments of its Chancellor (Jain, 2009) declare that the University aims to produce graduates that are "human resources as per the requirements of industry and the society" but who live by Jain ethical principles: "Right Philosophy, Right Knowledge and Right Conduct" (Jain, 2009, p. 1). The Vice Chancellor also emphasises the aspiration that, while graduates will possess technical expertise, they will gain an enhanced moral and ethical foundation, the better to serve society (Mittal, 2009).

	Interior	Exterior
	Interior Individual / Personal	Individual Exterior
Individual	"Enlightenment of the individual's heart, mind and soul is necessary for harmonious development of the society" (Jain, 2009).	Graduates are socially relevant, technically competent and professionally sound... Professionals who have a global perspective. Critically Aware: Our endeavour is to impart knowledge and develop critical skills necessary to succeed both in professional and personal life.
	Interior Social	Exterior Social
Collective	Empowerment for the Community: "Empowering youth to think beyond self by building an educational system that ... helps to cultivate values such as empathy, humility and compassion." (Mittal, 2009).	Internationally recognized as a premier institution of excellence providing quality education, research and consultancy services to the global society. Relevant to industry – industry led.

Table 9. AQAL Analysis of Teerthanker Mahaveer University's Graduate Qualities

AQAL analysis of TMU's ambitions for its graduates emphasises self-development but its goal is the production of professionals and this is how it would be recognized (Table 9). However, it is notable how even its Individual Exterior, employability-related goals are couched in terms used by the Western Universities for Interior goals, while its Collective Interior goals show the very strong influence of its religious roots. The terms 'humility' and 'compassion' do not feature strongly in any of the other Graduate Attribute statements. However, intuitively, both would seem very beneficial from the global citizenship perspective.

Discussion

Writing this, we are conscious of having broken several unwritten rules of Western discourse on education. First, is the discourse that the best universities – the ones with all of the answers are those of the West. Second, is the discourse that higher education in India, and indeed across the developing world, is battling with low standards and has little to offer the Western world. This paper is about global citizenship, not citizenship defined in narrow Western terms, and achieving this must be a concerted effort that brings forth the best from all of our world's many cultures and traditions.

AQAL analysis highlights the differences in the ways that these six universities consider their roles in the production of graduate attributes. The two, certainly atypical, Indian Universities emphasise the self-development of the individual and, self-consciously, dream of their graduates making a special contribution to the outside world. The four, not very atypical, Western universities focus on the employer perspective of what their graduates will be able to do – the Individual Exterior Quadrant – and their approach seems to involve molding and training more than allowing their learners to self-develop. These concerns show signs of being moderated to acknowledge the wishes of their social contexts. There is a secondary focus on the Collective Interior attributes that dominated our first table (Table 2; Haigh &

Clifford, 2010; Haigh, 2008). However, despite the furore that afflicts these Universities' desire to market themselves as distinctive brands (Twitchell, 2004), their Graduate Attribute statements have little to say about the role their graduates should play in the outside world.

So, taking Wilber's quadrants in turn we see that the most populated quadrants are those of the Individual Exterior and the Collective Interior. The Individual Exterior graduate statements emphasise an array of personal attributes and skills that range from the academic assertion of literacies and particular areas of knowledge or expertise, through qualities such as capability, professionalism and critical awareness, all with an underlying focus on employability. Only India's Visva-Bharati University emphasises aesthetical appreciation and commitment to social causes.

The Collective Interior quadrant is the area of good citizenship and community engagement. Strathclyde is content to offer its students a global outlook without any reference to direct engagement with communities, while the other universities mention different levels of engagement with local, national, global and professional communities. Melbourne aspires to produce leaders and change agents, and specifically mentions involvement with global sustainability, while Wollongong stresses professional values and ethics. TMU seeks to empower students with values such as empathy, humility and compassion while Oxford Brookes explicitly aspires to develop responsible citizens active in issues of equity, social justice, sustainability and the reduction of prejudice, stereotyping and discrimination. Visva-Bharati specifically wants its graduates to contribute to world peace. For academic staff with less than Barrie's (2006) 'enabling conception' of graduate attributes, many of these ideas would certainly be challenging.

In the Interior Individual quadrant, the arena of self development, TMU and Visva-Bharati University explicitly target individual spiritual growth or enlightenment, areas not alluded to by the UK and Australian universities. The University of Melbourne and Oxford Brookes emphasise critical self-awareness, while Wollongong and Oxford Brookes refer to independent thinking, and Strathclyde champions accepting ethical responsibilities.

The final quadrant, the Collective Social Exterior, collects statements about how a University would like to be seen as a whole, which is not necessarily something incorporated in statements of graduate attributes but more usually spelled out on the university's 'About Us' pages. In our examples, Strathclyde aims to be a place of useful learning, while Wollongong strives to be a place of international standing and TMU wishes to offer a world-class education. Oxford Brookes's visions is to have an international reputation for teaching excellence and research and to educate citizens for 'lives of consequence' (Oxford Brookes, 2010b), to have strong links in their local region through business and industry, and also to strive for a global reach. Melbourne portrays itself as a global research powerhouse. In contrast Visva-Bharati sees itself as an international centre to meld East and West.

All of this indicates a healthy diversity both within and between universities. Understandably, there is great concern about graduates being employable and being successful, especially in the professions. However, emphasis is also given to graduates being influential once employed and being committed to solving social and economic concerns of the community. It is heartening to see that some attention is paid to the development of learners' interior personal qualities, including taking personal responsibility both for their own learning, the needs of others, and their World.

Here we are concerned about what the analysis tells us about education for global citizenship. The literature churns ideas of global citizenship being about humanity and social justice and extends into environmental sustainability and Deep Ecology (Davies, 2006; Berry, 1999). However, most definitions accept that it includes the development of a set of personal sensitivities, personal responsibilities and a personal commitment to action as an essential part of that citizenship role. Considering the graduate attributes analysed above, Strathclyde's statement 'Global in outlook, thinking internationally' merely refers to students gaining an international outlook. There is no reference to how their graduates should use global perspective or any expectation that they will act upon it. Melbourne opts for a fuller statement of 'Active global citizens, accepting social and civic responsibilities, being an advocate for environmental sustainability, with a high regard for human rights, equity and ethics'. This indicates a full commitment to the ideal of an active global citizenship concerned with the full agenda of sustainability, human rights, equity and ethics, as also expressed eloquently by Visva-Bharati University. Oxford Brookes's concept of active global citizenship extends these issues through the notion of interculturality. Additionally, Oxford Brookes offers a further dimension, 'Confidence to question one's own values and those of others responsibly and ethically'. This embraces the idea of personal self awareness and the ability to articulate one's own values and the reasons for them, and to be able to engage responsibly in ethical debates with others.

In our previous paper (Haigh & Clifford, 2011), we argued that personal development and well-being were essential facets of global citizenship. There is a difference between 'knowing' your duties and obligations and acting the role of the responsible citizen (whether at a local or national level), and having a personal commitment to, and belief in, our common humanity and the necessity to be proactive in terms of justice, equity and sustainability globally. In order to be a responsible, active global citizen one needs to have the capacity for self-reflection and critique about one's own culture, the ability to see oneself as a member of a multicultural nation and diverse world and to be able to imagine sympathetically the different lives of others (Nussbaum, 2007).

Morin (2001) argues that the basic function of education is to develop the intellectual capacity of individuals to promote world understanding. Our analysis suggests that our personal, spiritual development, (the Individual Interior area), is still weakly developed especially in the Western university graduate attribute statements (cf. Barnett, 2006; Popovic et al., 2010).

Conclusion

Here, we present an analysis of the graduate attribute aspirations published by six universities from India, Australia and the UK. Although a small sample, they provide, we hope, a thought-provoking snapshot of the way in which different universities conceive the attributes they wish for their graduates. In particular, we have sought to illustrate how these universities differ in the emphases they place on, first, how they are seen as universities (Collective Exterior) and how their graduates (Individual Exterior) should be seen by the outside world and, second, how they see themselves contributing to social processes (Collective Interior) and how they hope their graduates will be developed as persons in their own right (Individual Interior).

These examples illustrate that all of the universities have a strong commitment to preparing students for the workforce (Individual Exterior) and that for Melbourne this includes preparing students to be leaders in their communities, while most others also emphasize entrepreneurial and professional skills. However, this is not as single-minded as some of the literature might imply (Yorke & Harvey, 2005). There is also a focus on a graduate's future place, involvement and commonly leadership roles in their local, national and global communities (Interior Collective): with universities such as Visva-Bharati University committing their graduates, explicitly, to the relief of social injustice; and TMU talking of social empowerment. Despite much rhetoric about personal awareness, ethical and moral responsibility, there is less emphasis in the Western universities on the development of Individual Interior qualities than in the aspirations expressed by the two, admittedly rather special, Indian Universities. However, almost all of the universities address the notion of global citizenship. Oxford Brookes University mentions interculturality and environmental sustainability, while Visva-Bharati University talks of peace building and promoting East-West understanding.

Although the assignment of statements to one or other quadrant in this analysis is not always clear cut, the contrast between the Western and non-Western universities highlights important cultural differences in the ways that graduate attributes are conceived and demonstrated and shows that there is much scope for cross-cultural learning. Possibly, the Indian universities explored might benefit from thinking more deeply about the Individual Exterior and their graduates employability skills. The Western universities might benefit from a clearer vision of their role in the wider world and their need to focus on helping their learners self-develop the ethical and empathic qualities that will help them become well-rounded, educated, global citizens.

We reflect that rhetoric about active global citizenship may not be sustainable without a co-commitment to the personal development of students and their sense of personal responsibility for others. Statements of graduate attributes may be a positive influence because they do help bring such issues to the surface. Such thoughts reopen our debate about where the fundamental attributes of a graduate lie – within their selves, their disciplinary skills (Clifford, 2009), in their capabilities or in what they do for society and the world; and, indeed, about what is the real purpose and value of higher education?

References

AEN (2011). *Rankings of Australian Universities*. Collingwood, Victoria: Australian Educational Network. Retrieved February 20, 2011, from **http://www.australian-universities.com/rankings/**

Agarwal, P. (2009). *Indian Higher Education: Envisioning the Future*. New Delhi: Sage.

Barnett, R. (2006). Graduate Attributes in an age of uncertainty. In S. Holland and P. Hager, *Graduate Attributes, Learning and Employability*. (pp. 49–65), Dordrecht: Springer.

Barrie, S.C. (2006). Understanding what we mean by generic attributes of graduates. *Higher Education, 51*(2), 215–241.

Berry, T.M. (1999). *The Great Work: Our Way into the Future*. New York: Belltower.

Clifford, V.A. (2009). Engaging the Disciplines in Internationalising the Curriculum, *International Journal of Academic Development, 14*(2), 133–143.

Davies, L. (2006). Global citizenship: abstraction or framework for action? *Educational Review, 58*(1), 5–25.

Delors, J. (1996). *Learning: The Treasure Within*. Paris: UNESCO.

Hager, P., & Holland, S. (2006). Introduction. In P. Hager & S. Holland (Eds.), *Graduate attributes, learning and employability*. (pp. 1–15). Dordrecht: Springer.

Haigh, M. (2008). Internationalisation, Planetary Citizenship and Higher Education Inc. Compare: *A Journal of Comparative Education, 38*(4), 427–449.

Haigh, M. (2005). Editorial: Geography and the EYCE (European Year of Citizenship through Education). *Journal of Geography in Higher Education, 29*(2), 173–182.

Haigh, M. & Clifford, V.A. (2010). Widening the Graduate Attribute Debate in Higher Education to Encompass Global Citizenship. *Brookes electronic Journal of Learning and Teaching, 2*(5), 1–10. Retrieved February 3, 2011 from **http://bejlt.brookes.ac.uk/article/widening_the_graduate_attribute _debate_a_higher_education_for_global_citize/**

Haigh, M & Clifford, V. (2011). Integral Vision: a multi-perspective approach to the recognition of Graduate Attributes. *Higher Education Research & Development, 13*(5), in press.

Harvey, L. (2005). Embedding and integrating employability. *New Directions for Institutional Research,* 128, 13–28.

Harvey, L. (2001). Defining and measuring employability. *Quality in Higher Education, 7*(2), 97–109.

Hill J. D. (2000). *Becoming a cosmopolitan: what it means to be a human being in the new millennium.* Lanham, MD: Rowman and Littlefield.

Inayatullah, S. (2010). *Spirituality as the Fourth Bottom Line.* Metafutures.org: articles. Retrieved February 20, 2011, from **http://www.metafuture.org/Articles/spirituality_bottom_line.htm.**

Jain, S. (2009) *Message of the Chancellor.* Mordabad, U.P., India, Teerthanker Mahaveer University. Retrieved February 20, 2011, from **http://www.tmu.ac.in/messagechancellor.htm**

Jain 'Sadak', J.P. (2005.) Introduction. In J.P. Jain 'Sadak', *Salvation through Self-Discipline: Niyamasara of Kundakunda* (pp. 1–153). New Delhi: Radient.

Marien, M. (2002). Futures studies in the 21st Century: a reality-based view. *Futures 34*(3–4), 261–281.

McKenzie, K.B., Christman, D.E, Hernandez, F., Fierro, E., Capper C.A., Dantley, M., González, M-L., Cambron-McCabe, N. & Scheurich, J.J. (2008) From the Field: A Proposal for Educating Leaders for Social Justice. *Educational Administration Quarterly, 44*(1), 111–138.

Milojeviè, I. (2005). *Educational Futures: Dominant and Contesting Visions.* London: Routledge.

Mittal, R.K. (2009). *Message of the Vice Chancellor.* Teerthanker Mahaveer University, Mordabad, U.P. Retrieved February 20, 2011, from **http://www.tmu.ac.in/messagevc.htm**

Morin, E. (2001). *Seven complex lessons in education for the future.* Paris: United Nations Educational, Scientific, and Cultural Organisation.

Nussbaum, M. (2007). Cultivating humanity and world citizenship. *Forum Futures 2007*, 37–40. Retrieved February 23, 2009, from **http://net.educause.edu/ir/library/pdf/ff0709s.pdf.**

Oxford Brookes University (2010a). *Strategy for Enhancing the Student Experience 2010–2015.* Retrieved February 20, 2011, from: **http://www.brookes.ac.uk/about/structure/2020/documents/sese2 010-15.pdf**

Oxford Brookes University (2010b). *Strategy 2020.* Retrieved April 19, 2010 from **http://www.brookes.ac.uk/about/structure/mission 2020**

Popovic, C., Lawton, R., Hill, A., Eland, J. & Morton, N. (2010). *Creating Future Proof Graduates: Final Report.* Birmingham City University, Birmingham & Higher Education Academy York. 49pp. Retrieved February 20, 2011, from **http://www.heacademy.ac.uk/assets/York/documents/ourwork/ntf s/projects/Creating_Future_Proof_Graduates_Final_report.doc.**

QAA (Scotland). (2007). *Graduates for the 21st century: integrating the enhancement themes.* Scottish Higher Education Enhancement Committee (SHEEC). Retrieved February 23, 2009, from **http://www.enhancementthemes.ac.uk/themes/ResearchTeaching /attributes.asp**

Ray, R.K. (2010). From the Vice-Chancellor. Santiniketan, Visva-Bharati University. Retrieved February 20, 2011, from **http://www.visva-bharati.ac.in/MessageFromVC/MessageFromVC.htm**

Tagore, S. (2008). Tagore's conception of cosmopolitanism: a reconstruction. *University of Toronto Quarterly, 77*(4), 1070–1084.

TMU (2010) *Teerthanker Mahaveer University: An Ultimate Destination for World Class Education.* Mordabad, U.P., India. Retrieved February 20, 2011, from **http://www.tmu.ac.in/**

Twitchell, J. B. (2004). *Branded Nation: The Marketing of Mega Church, College Inc and Museumworld.* New York: Simon & Schuster.

University of Melbourne (2008). *What is the Melbourne Model?* Retrieved February 20, 2011, from **http://futurestudents.unimelb.edu.au/courses/melbourne-model**

University of Melbourne (2007). *Attributes of the Melbourne graduate.* Retrieved February 20, 2011, from **http://www.unimelb.edu.au/about/attributes.html.**

University of Strathclyde (nd). *Development, jobs and careers.* Retrieved February 20, 2011, from **http://www.strath.ac.uk/learnteach/learning/ developmentjobscareers**

University of Strathclyde (2010). *Graduates for the 21st Century.* University of Strathclyde News Release 20 .10.2010. Retrieved February 20, 2011, from **http://www.strath.ac.uk/press/newsreleases/ headline_336696_en.html**

University of Wollongong (2010). *UOW Graduate Qualities.* Retrieved February 20, 2011, from **http://www.uow.edu.au/about/teaching/qualities/index.html**

University of Wollongong in Dubai (nd). *Graduate Qualities.* Retrieved February 18, 2011, from **http://www.uowdubai.ac.ae/aboutus/details.php?sec=1,7**

Visva-Bharati University (2006). *About Visva-Bharati.* Santiniketan, Visva-Bharati University. Retrieved February 17, 2011, from **http://www.visva-bharati.ac.in/SiteMap/SiteMap.htm**

Wilber, K. (2006). *Integral Spirtuality: A Startling New Role for Religion in the Modern and Postmodern World.* Boston: Integral Books.

Wilber, K. (2001). *A Theory of Everything: An Integral Vision for Business, Politics, Science and Spirituality.* Boston: Shambala.

Woolmer, C. (2009). *Employability.* TALQIC (Teaching and Learning Quality Improvement Committee). Glasgow, University of Strathclyde. Retrieved August 29, 2010, from **http://ewds.strath.ac.uk/Articles/tabid/2552/articleType/ArticleView/articleId/54/Graduate-Attributes.aspx.**

Yorke, M. & Harvey, L. (2005). Graduate attributes and their development. *New Directions for Institutional Research 128,* 41–58,

Part 2

Research on practice

Research in internationalisation of the curriculum for global citizenship: Where do we stand?

6

Catherine Montgomery and Valerie Clifford

Introduction

This book presents 12 chapters of policy, research and practice studies that concentrate on the theme of Internationalisation of the Curriculum (IoC) with a focus on global citizenship. Each one presents a unique and distinctive perspective on this multi-faceted field. The purpose of this chapter is to pause for a moment from reading the chapters themselves, reflect on the sort of research that is about to be presented in the second part of the book, and contextualise this in the wider field. The chapter will highlight a number of aspects of the research from the second section of the book. The relationship of the research with the broader picture of research in Internationalisation of the Curriculum will also be considered. In this way we hope to emphasise the variety of research approaches in the field and identify particular aspects of research in IoC that may merit further attention, encouraging others to research in these areas.

Like all research fields, research in Internationalisation of the Curriculum for global citizenship has distinctive aspects; and, especially being related to learning, the field has a strong link with practice. The relationship between research and teaching is a crucial one, and is particularly acute in IoC research, which can be seen to be at the centre of questions relating to the roles and responsibilities of higher education. In addition to this, research in Internationalisation of the Curriculum spans all disciplines and is embedded in a particular range of cultural, political and social contexts. In this chapter we look firstly at research that has been carried out in the last two decades in the field of IoC; secondly, we focus on the current research that is being carried out including the contribution made by the chapters of this book; and finally, we raise some issues that we view as crucial to future research in this field.

Past Research in the Field of IoC

Disciplines and their associated elements are far from being rigid and unchanging but evolve over time as social and intellectual constructs (Repko, 2008). Research in IoC is such an evolving construct, and has begun to emerge as a research field in its own right. Whilst IoC may be associated with more recent research fields such as internationalisation or globalisation that have emerged strongly in recent decades, it has also begun to accumulate central concepts and organising theories, and to embrace certain methods of investigation that are embedding it as a part of disciplinary study (Repko, 2008). Some of these concepts and theories are considered in this part of the chapter, with a particular focus on the methodological approaches of recent decades, the link between research and practice, and the engagement with multiple perspectives embedded in this field.

A methodological home?

Clifford and Montgomery (this volume) and Green and Mertova (this volume) note that understandings of IoC are still in their infancy and that more research is needed. However, methodological approaches to understanding internationalisation have changed and developed over the last two decades. The choice of methodological approaches in this research tells us about the underlying assumptions that are being made about knowledge and ways of understanding. Also, the sorts of questions that are being asked in IoC research provide important insights into the areas that researchers have felt are significant.

During the 1990s and early 2000s there was a predominance of quantitative studies which were often quite small-scale and used inventories or questionnaires. Some of these quantitative instruments aimed to 'measure' aspects of students 'international' development, competence or sensitivity in intercultural interaction; for example, the Intercultural Development Inventory (Hammer, Bennett & Wiseman, 2003), and the Socio-cultural Adaptation Scale (Searle & Ward, 1990). These inventories were also available on a commercial basis, lending a market-research orientation to this area of research in internationalisation. Some of these scales also claimed to be effective methods of developing or evaluating internationalised curricula or of charting 'adjustment' during cross-cultural transitions (Rogers & Ward, 1993). During the 2000s, however, there was a marked turn towards more qualitative approaches to research in IoC, and this was part of the distinct movement in social sciences research in general towards more interpretive, postmodern and criticalist practices (Guba & Lincoln, 2005). A nuanced range of different qualitative approaches have been emerging in the field, including a broad range of case study approaches (Wai Lo, 2009; Chapman & Pyvis, 2007), autobiographical narrative inquiry (Trahar, 2011), ethnographies (Hou, Montgomery & McDowell, 2011), longitudinal studies of experience (Adelman, 2004) and methodologies that are practice-focused such as action research (Peidong & Laidlaw, 2006). This is not to suggest that there is a polarised development in research methodologies in IoC, and it is important to note that quantitative studies have continued to be done, with Harrison's (forthcoming) large-scale quantitative study of attitudes to intercultural interaction being an interesting example. This development in the range of research methodologies being used has begun to promote an emergent, non-positivist orientation, creating a context in which it is more common for studies to be challenged by proponents of contending paradigms (Guba & Lincoln, 2005).

The development of this variety in research methodologies is a positive move towards generating a more multi-faceted range of perspectives on IoC, but also raises the question of whether too much diversity in methodologies and disciplinary contexts may be a barrier to developing the concepts and organising theories that will enable IoC to move forward as a discipline in its own right. Recent volumes of research in the field have been collections of chapters (Jones, 2010; Jones & Brown, 2007, this volume) and it should be noted that whilst coherent collections of research present a much-needed range of perspectives, there is also a need for a coherent linking between the pockets of excellence in IoC research, so that progress with central concepts and organising theories unifying the field can be made.

Another important aspect of IoC research which tells us about research in the field is the sorts of questions that have been asked in the last two decades. The questions that preoccupy researchers are just as important as (and are embedded in) the methodologies that they use to answer their questions. As with the methodologies, questions have developed and changed along with ways of thinking in the field. In the late 1980s and during the 1990s there was a preponderance of questions that asked how mobile, in-coming international students should adjust to the curriculum and its environment (Furnham, 1997; Black, Mendenhall & Oddou, 1991), and the focus of research appeared to be on 'the international student' (Kinnell, 1990). Many questions were also asked about 'culture shock' and culture or 'learning styles' of international students which were seen as the concepts which influenced learning. During the late 1990s and into 2000s, however, the focus of questioning appeared to shift away from adjustment in the international student and began to centre on the need to adapt the curriculum. Research began to interrogate the curriculum itself and to ask how the 'home' context, the 'home' student and the 'home' curriculum can and should adapt to internationalisation, as noted by the idea of 'internationalisation at home' (Teekens, 2000). Alongside this, an allied research literature on sustainability emerged (Haigh, 2008; Bourn, 2011). Research questions also began to be asked about pedagogy and how the design of the teaching, learning and assessment environment might be influential in promoting or impeding international learning (Montgomery, 2009; Carroll & Li, 2008). This volume also represents a further move forwards in its questions about how learning beyond the 'classroom' (variously called informal learning or 'service' learning) can contribute to educating global citizens (Caruana, this volume; Montgomery, this volume). The focus on research in global citizenship has also developed, and continues to grow, alongside increasing interest in the value of graduate attributes (Barrie, 2004; Clifford & Haigh, this volume). There are also indications that academic service and citizenship more widely are developing areas of research interest (Brew & Akerlind, 2009). In addition to questions on the enhancement of learning and the curriculum, questions have begun to be asked about university 'policy' on internationalisation, with a focus on quality assurance and systems (Van Damme, 2001).

Overall, the rise in prominence of research in IoC is evidence of the fact that academics are actively investigating this field, and are not passively accepting the structures and situations in which they find themselves as a result of globalisation: and through their research, they are taking on the mantle of global citizens (Brew & Akerlind, 2009).

Research and practice

Humboldt, who is often seen as the 'father' of the modern university, proposed that the unity of teaching and research was a formative principle of the university (Thornton, 2009). Much recent research in the field of higher education as a whole has focused on the relationship between research and practice and has involved questioning what is

understood by higher learning and the nature of 'the academy'.
Understanding the relationship between research and teaching involves
asking substantial questions about the roles and responsibilities of
higher education institutions, about the nature of academic work, the
kinds of disciplinary knowledge that are developed, and by whom, and
the relationships between students and teachers (Brew, 2006, p. 3).
These are also questions that are seen as significant in the field of IoC.
The synergy between research and practice is at the foreground in IoC
partly because the researchers who engage in this research are
themselves practitioners who are often questioning aspects of their own
context in the light of internationalisation and globalisation. In
addition to this, many approaches to linking research and teaching
involve a focus on collaboration between staff and students, and entail
rethinking power relations in higher education by viewing students
and staff as part of inclusive knowledge-building communities (ibid).
These collaborative, mutually formative social environments are those
that are often espoused for pedagogy in the field of IoC.

Barnett (2000) argues that research needs to produce socially useful
knowledge and have the power to transform those who engage in it.
Maxwell (1984, cited in Brew, 2006, p. 172) notes that the purpose of
academic research should be to solve the complex, current problems
of living. Much research in IoC and global citizenship asks how we
can integrate this into our teaching so that the role of the university
can be to educate graduates who will engage in this problem solving.
This chapter demonstrates that these sorts of views of the relationship
between research and practice are crucial cornerstones of this field.

Current Research in Internationalisation of the Curriculum

We now focus on current research in the field, and consider the
contribution of the research presented in this book to new and
innovative ways of thinking about Internationalisation of the
Curriculum.

Narrative and reflective methodologies

Denzin and Lincoln note that there is no 'correct' telling of an event. 'Each telling, like light hitting a crystal, reflects a different perspective on this incident' (2005, p. 6). The chapters in the research and practice section of this book reflect such a range of different ways of telling stories, concepts and ideas about Internationalisation of the Curriculum and global citizenship. All the chapters follow a broadly qualitative approach: but this does not mean that these are the 'best' ways to understand IoC, but simply that this approach tells particular kinds of stories about the 'event'. Qualitative research covers a wide range of perspectives and is difficult to define but is a set of interpretive activities which emphasises no single methodological practice over another (ibid). All research is interpretive as it is guided by the researcher's beliefs and feelings about the world and how it should be understood and studied (Denzin & Lincoln, 2005). There are particular methods associated with interpretive and qualitative inquiry, however, and some of these are reflected in these chapters. Many of the accounts presented here aim to confront the complexities of the everyday social world and try to show this world in action and embed their findings in it (Denzin & Lincoln, 2005, p. 12).

The emphasis on narrative inquiry and reflection in the chapters in the second part of the book attests to the fact that this approach to inquiry is 'flourishing' and knows the world through the stories that are told about it (Denzin & Lincoln, 2005, p. 641). Narrative is becoming increasingly recognised as a valid and viable way to explore the complex nature of teaching and learning (Zhong, 2010). Chase defines narrative as an

> amalgam of interdisciplinary lenses, diverse disciplinary approaches and both traditional and innovative methods – all revolving around an interest in biographical particulars as narrated by the one who lives them. (2005, p. 651).

Narrative inquiry presents itself as a useful way of telling the stories of IoC and global citizenship as it centres on drawing out diverse perspectives and accessing the complexity of lived experience. In this section Holliday presents ethnographic narratives that uncover his own complicity in creating stereotype, and he notes that no single piece of data would have been sufficient to make this point. Montgomery et al. use three socially constructed narratives of student experience, drawing on autoethnographic methods and attempting to present the flow of thoughts and meanings of the student experience with some immediacy. Davis employs a personal reflective narrative that aims to provide insight into her own journey through the culture and context of her discipline. Montgomery and Spiro's chapter presents teachers' 'hidden' narratives of their personal and professional motivations for engaging in border crossings. It is in this book's predominant use of both narrative and reflective approaches to IoC research that part of the originality and innovation of the collection lies.

Critical and radical research positions

It is interesting to note that the majority of the chapters in the book are written by researchers in the UK. This reflects the geographical location of the conference that generated the chapters in this book. However, as argued above, it is not necessarily the context in which the research is carried out but the values and perspectives which are being presented that are important. A number of the chapters in this section aim to present a non-Western perspective and aim for a critical stance on the practices of Western universities. Holliday's chapter is crucial to this book's questioning of the idea of the 'West', for example, and the promotion of a critical position on understanding our interactions with internationalisation. His emphasis on the idea of critical cosmopolitanism underlines the point that cultural boundaries are imagined and constructed in an unequal world, and that many notions that we assume are shared – such as equal rights, universalism, humanism, and democracy – do not extend beyond the borders of the 'West'. This critical stance on cultural assumptions is reflected in other chapters in the book. Davis critically reflects on the discipline-specific term of 'rehabilitation' and charts the development of her realisation that this is also not a universal concept. The critical positions taken in these chapters are central to the philosophy of this book: in 'Western' institutions we need to adopt self-critical, questioning and potentially radical approaches to understanding our interactions with internationalisation.

Holliday draws out a particular strand of the conceptualisation of global citizenship; namely, cultural global politics as it is acted out in the everyday academic and institutional domains of the university. He provides a critical perspective on ideas of multiculturalism and cosmopolitanism, underlining the need for critical cultural awareness in our interactions with others. He suggests that for global citizenship to develop, there needs to be change to the way in which Western institutions, pedagogies and everyday perceptions construct the foreign. If critical cosmopolitanism is to work and thrive, we need to at once normalise our interactions with the other but also understand ourselves and our tendency to construct the 'foreign other'.

Davis provides an example of how this might play out in practice as she reflects on her journey in the course of her doctoral study where her developing understandings of the cultural sensitivity of the concept of 'rehabilitation' leads her to attempt to reshape and adapt her curricula to students' prospects and destinations. Davis charts the development of her realisation of her own construction of stereotypes and how this development was embedded in the learning processes of her doctoral study.

Montgomery and Spiro present a collection of poetry brought together during the academic conference which generated the chapters in this book. They reflect on this collection, which provided an opportunity for staff to 'write themselves' into the research process of the conference as they sought to understand the personal meanings associated with becoming a global citizen. The chapter considers these insights, and the way learning can be enhanced and expressed through the medium of creative writing as distinct from more traditional academic discourse.

Montgomery focuses 'at home' and considers the connections that students make between informal learning activity and their university studies. Here student engagement in the informal curriculum of activity beyond the classroom is seen as contributing to students' understanding of their academic discipline and its role in a globalised world, as well as to their own development as socially and ethically rounded graduates or global citizens.

Caruana's conceptualisation of global citizenship analyses the challenges, controversies and tensions involved in research in this field. Caruana outlines how global citizenship education requires opportunities to develop qualities and insights that transcend narrow visions of learning in higher education. Caruana notes that service-learning and community volunteering offer distinct possibilities in delivering the curriculum and pedagogy to provide for global citizenship education in higher education, but that there is relatively little research to evaluate these kinds of interventions. This leads us to consider what sorts of emphases may be appropriate as we move towards Internationalisation of the Curriculum for global citizenship.

Future IoC Research

Developing 'respect for different cultures of inquiry'
(Cousins, 2009, p. 9).

All research and its analysis comes from particular standpoints, and the cultural context in which research is carried out is also crucially influential (Charmaz, 2005). The nature of research in IoC means that it is essential that different cultural perspectives are included and acknowledged. Research 'cultures' develop at particular points in time, and these are influenced by the contemporary political, socio-cultural and contextual agendas (McNay, 2009). For example, current trends towards a more 'entrepreneurial research culture', where research funding provided by industry or research councils governs whether and how a project or issue is approached, result in research agendas being 'commercially' or externally driven (Thornton, 2009, p. 23). As mentioned above, research in IoC is at the centre of such a complex set of performative, political and economic tensions. In addition to this, there are other contextual factors that have a powerful influence on the nature of research in the field. There are many of these but two are fore-grounded here: the significance of the tensions between 'Western' and 'non-Western' perspectives and the influence of linguistic contexts.

It comes as no surprise to note that the countries in which IoC research is carried out are predominantly 'Western' (Trahar, 2011) and this identifies internationalisation as a Western construct that is sometimes seen as a 'cover for creeping Westernisation' (Merrick, 2000, p. xii, cited in Trahar, 2011, p. 20). Trahar notes:

> I am aware that the western academy can be seen as a colonising institution (Carey, 2004), especially in its subtle treatment of those who do not belong to its dominant culture. (2011, p. 20).

Thus the idea of what counts as 'quality' educational experience is embedded in this Western perspective, and the predominance of the research contexts being 'Western' means that IoC research does not represent an even or completely diverse picture of the nature of internationalisation and global citizenship across the globe. Indeed the terms themselves are culture-specific. So this begs the question of what it means to present a 'Western' or 'non-Western' point of view. The construct of 'the West' itself is fluid and is a misnomer in that it is not a geographical division but an ideological one. Trouillot notes:

> "the West" is always a fiction, an exercise in global legitimation…Thus the West has never had a fixed content, nor is it an unchanging site… It can absorb parts of Eastern Europe or Latin America, and more recently Japan not because of any feature common to these areas but rather depending on who else is being excluded. (2003, p. 2).

Because the West is not fixed in content or cultures it means that IoC research that is located in 'non-Western' contexts may still present 'Western' ideology and vice versa. It may not be true to say that researchers who carry out their work in a 'Western' location or working for 'Western' institutions will present solely 'Western' views. At the same time researchers who are culturally and politically located in 'non-Western' contexts may express views that align more closely with 'Western' ideologies. It is the cultural perspectives and values of the researcher that exert powerful influence on questions being asked and ways of finding answers about internationalisation, curriculum and global citizenship. A crucial element then, for moving forward in IoC research, is the development of a 'respect for different cultures of inquiry' (Cousins, 2009, p. 9).

More research that incorporates 'non-Western' perspectives is crucial to the development of IoC. Haigh represents a notable example of a Western researcher's attempts at presenting non-Western perspectives on Internationalisation of the Curriculum (Haigh, 2008). He constructed a curriculum based on Indian philosophy to provide home students with a new perspective on learning. In addition to this, it is not uncommon in this field for 'Western' researchers and 'non-Western' researchers to collaborate on inquiry and in publication (Peidong & Laidlaw, 2006; Salehi-Sangari & Foster, 1999). In light of the slippery notions of culture, context and perspective, the future of IoC may require more studies that incorporate a 'critical' analysis, bearing in mind that 'criticality' itself may be seen as a 'Western' value (Vandermensbrugghe, 2004).

Another crucial aspect of the context of research in IoC is that it is predominantly written in English. The use of English as a lingua franca is closely tied to processes of globalisation and it can be seen as a language which poses a threat, represents power and control, or alternatively provides opportunity for new forms of resistance or appropriation of identity (Pennycook, 2007, p. 5). Global political initiatives such as the emphasis on the citation index in judging the impact of research more widely have meant that publication in native languages has reduced dramatically in favour of publication in (American) English as a route into politically-valued international journals (McNay, 2009). As language frames thought, this new rise in linguistic imperialism can be seen as part of the 'Western' colonisation of research structures (ibid). The influence of English as the dominant language of research means that many diverse viewpoints are silenced and non-English speakers are marginalised. English speakers are also disadvantaged by a lack of access to multiple viewpoints that might unsettle the hegemony of dominant ways of 'reading' the world (Subedi, 2010). Wai Lo writes:

> The hegemony of the English-speaking systems in the academic world gives a forceful reason for academics from non-English speaking countries to abandon writing and publishing in indigenous languages (2009, p. 734).

Thus research in this field and more generally can be seen as a significant site of struggle between the 'West' and the Other, with many 'indigenous' researchers maintaining that marginalised voices are still excluded and a 'racialised research industry' persists (Asmar, Ripeka Mercia & Page, 2009, p. 147). Research in IoC particularly needs to hear these marginalised voices so that the field can move forward with collaborative and culturally appropriate approaches that 'transcend potential barriers' (ibid).

Credibility, validity and ethics

The discussion above relating to 'Western' and 'non-Western' perspectives raises the question of how credible and valid is research in IoC. According to Denzin and Lincoln (2005) the times of claiming that research (particularly research regarding the 'other') is value-free are over. They note that:

> Today researchers struggle to develop situational and transsituational ethics that apply to all forms of the research act and its human-to-human relationships. We no longer have the option of deferring the decolonization project (2005, p. 22).

In light of this, as we go forward with IoC research, credibility, validity and ethics will be crucial considerations. An important aspect of the credibility and validity of research in this field will be whether all 'stakeholders'' views are taken into account, and the critical questioning of 'Western' perspectives is key to this. The sorts of collaborative and cogenerative inquiry described above and in some chapters of this book are examples of attempts to do this. One of the challenges in involving all stakeholders, however, is ensuring that this is done ethically and that others' voices are not changed or coloured by interpretation of the researcher. The student narratives presented by Montgomery et al (this volume) are an example of an attempt to include the voice of students, sometimes ironically marginalised in the consideration of their learning.

In addition to involving all stakeholder perspectives, future research in IoC must be robust in its processes. The strong link between research and practice enacted through practitioners-as-researcher has been presented here as a positive aspect of research in this field. However, this link can also lead to research processes being carried out in a less than rigorous order, with ideas and data drawn from observation in practice leading inquiry without prior planning of the research and evaluation processes, and with ethical considerations of participant consent and access to data being dealt with belatedly and sometimes unsatisfactorily. It is important that all research into practice is rigorous and ethical. According to Denzin and Lincoln (2005) there are five phases in the research process, beginning with the acknowledgement of the researcher as a multicultural subject, identification of paradigms and research strategies, adoption of methods of collection and analysis and finally, and crucially for IoC, the understanding of the practices and politics of interpretation and evaluation. The experience of developing this book has underlined for us the need for such phases to be followed in order that research in IoC and global citizenship can be seen as a robust strand of disciplinary research in its own right.

Conclusion

Critical postmodern research paradigms motivate researchers to 'construct their perception of the world anew, not just in random ways but in a manner that undermines what appears natural, that opens to question what appears obvious' (Kincheloe & McLaren, 2005, p. 306). There is a need to locate research in IoC in this transformative praxis that leads to the rethinking of the role of higher education in influencing students' and staff understandings of global citizenship. The chapters of this book acknowledge the need for university education to develop a critical conscience. The research here attests to the need to reject a compromised view of global citizenship and ask searching questions through research about how what is, has come to be; whose interests are served by particular institutional arrangements; and where our own frames of reference come from. There is a need to be critical in an age of globalisation, otherwise performativity and marketisation will prevail: and this underlines the importance of continuing to develop IoC and global citizen research.

The range of disciplines in which IoC is embedded identifies it as being situated in 'contested terrain' and sometimes located in spaces between disciplines, mainly as a result of the fact that it addresses problems or questions that are the focus of several disciplines (Repko, 2008, p. 6). The challenge for IoC research is to be able to communicate across these different disciplinary contexts in order to build up a shared understanding of concepts and practice, 'building on the shoulders of giants rather than rediscovering the wheel in separate local communities' (Brew, 2006, p. 104).

References

Adelman, C. (2004). Global preparedness of pre-9/11 college graduates: what US longitudinal studies say. *Tertiary education and management, 10*(3), 243–260.

Asmar, C., Ripeka Mercia, O. & Page, S. (2009). 'You do it from your core': priorities, perceptions and practices of research among Indigenous academics in Australian and New Zealand universities. In A. Brew & L. Lucas (Eds.) *Academic Research and Researchers* (pp. 146–161). Maidenhead McGraw Hill: Open University Press.

Barnett, R. (2000). *Realising the university: In an age of supercomplexity.* Buckingham. SRHE Open University Press.

Barrie S.C. (2004). A research-based approach to generic graduate attributes policy. *Higher Education Research and Development. 23*(3), 261–275.

Black, J.S., Mendenhall, M. & Oddou, G. (1991). Towards a comprehensive model of international adjustment: an integration of multiple theoretical perspectives. *Academy of Management Review, 16*(2), 291–317.

Bourn, D. (2011). From Internationalisation to Global Perspectives, *Higher Education Research and Development, 30*(5), in press.

Brew, A. (2006). *Research and teaching: beyond the divide*. Basingstoke: Palgrave Macmillan.

Brew, A. & Akerlind, G.S. (2009). Conclusions: directions for future research. In Brew, A. & Lucas, L. (Eds.) *Academic Research and Researchers* (pp. 204–219). Maidenhead McGraw Hill: Open University Press.

Carroll, J. & Li, R. (2008, June). *Assessed group work in culturally diverse groups: is normative guidance useful in addressing students' worries about grades?* Paper presented at Using informal and formal curricula to improve interaction between international and home students. Centre for International Curriculum Inquiry and Networking Conference, Oxford Brookes University, Oxford, UK.

Chapman, A. & Pyvis, D.H. (2007). Why university students choose an international education: a case study in Malaysia. *International Journal of Educational Development, 27*(2), 235–246.

Chase, S.E. (2005). Narrative inquiry: multiple lenses, approaches, voices. In N.K. Denzin & Y.S. Lincoln (Eds). *The Sage Handbook of Qualitative Research* (3rd Edition) (pp. 651–681). Thousand Oaks, California: Sage.

Charmaz, K. (2005). Grounded theory in the 21st Century: Applications for advancing Social Justice Studies. In N.K. Denzin & Y.S. Lincoln (Eds). *The Sage Handbook of Qualitative Research* (3rd Edition) (pp. 507–537). Thousand Oaks, California: Sage.

Cousin, G. (2009). *Researching learning in higher education*. London: Routledge.

Denzin, N.K. and Lincoln, Y.S. (2005). Introduction: the discipline and practice of qualitative research. In N.K. Denzin & Y.S. Lincoln (Eds). *The Sage Handbook of Qualitative Research* (3rd Edition) (pp. 1–33). Thousand Oaks, California: Sage.

Furnham, A. (1997). *Being an overseas student*. London: Routledge.

Guba, E.G. & Lincoln, Y.S. (2005). Paradigmatic controversies, contradictions and emerging confluences. In N.K. Denzin & Y.S. Lincoln (Eds). *The Sage Handbook of Qualitative Research* (3rd Edition) (pp. 191–217). Thousand Oaks, California: Sage.

Haigh, M. (2008). Internationalisation, planetary citizenship and Higher Education Inc. *Compare: a Journal of Comparative and International Education. 38*(4), 427–440.

Hammer, R.M., Bennet, M.J. & Wiseman, R. (2003). Measuring intercultural sensitivity: the Intercultural Development Inventory. *International Journal of Intercultural Relations. 27,* (2003), 421–443.

Harrison, N. (forthcoming). Investigating the impact of personality and early life experiences on intercultural interaction in internationalised universities. Accepted for publication in *International Journal of Intercultural Relations.*

Hou, J., Montgomery, C. & McDowell, L. (2011). Transition in Chinese – British Higher Education Articulation Programmes: Closing the Gap between East and West? In J. Ryan (Ed.) *China's higher education: reform and internationalisation.* (pp. 97–114). London: Routledge.

Jones, E. (2010). *Internationalisation and the Student Voice. Higher Education Perspectives.* Oxford: Routledge

Jones, E. & Brown, S. (2007). *Internationalising Higher Education.* Oxford: Routledge.

Kincheloe, J.L. & McLaren, P. (2005). Rethinking critical theory and qualitative research. In N.K. Denzin & Y.S. Lincoln (Eds). *The Sage Handbook of Qualitative Research* (3rd Edition) (pp. 303–343). Thousand Oaks, California: Sage.

Kinnell, M. (1990). *The learning experiences of international students.* Buckingham: SRHE.

McNay, I. (2009). Research quality assessment: objectives, approaches, responses and consequences. In A. Brew & L. Lucas (Eds.) *Academic Research and Researchers* (pp. 35–54). Maidenhead McGraw Hill: Open University Press.

Montgomery, C. (2009). A Decade of Internationalisation: has it influenced students' views of cross-cultural group work at university? *Journal of Studies in International Education, 13*(2) 256–270.

Peidong, L. & Laidlaw, M. (2006). Collaborative enquiry, action research and curriculum development in rural China: how can we facilitate a process of educational change? *Action Research, 4*(3), 333–350.

Pennycook, A. (2007). *Global Englishes and transcultural flows*. Oxford: Routledge.

Ramsden, P. (2003). *Learning to teach in higher education* (2nd Edition). London: Routledge Falmer.

Repko, A.F. (2008). *Interdisciplinary research: process and theory*. London: Sage

Rogers, J. and Ward, C. (1993). Expectation–experience discrepancies and psychological adjustment during cross-cultural re-entry. *International Journal of Intercultural Relations. 17*(1993), 185–196.

Salehi-Sangari, E. & Forster, T. (1999). Curriculum internationalisation: a comparative study in Iran and Sweden. *Journal of Marketing, 33*(7), 760–772.

Searle, W. & Ward, C. (1990). The prediction of psychological and sociocultural adjustment during cross-cultural transitions. International *Journal of Intercultural Relations. 12*, 61–71.

Subedi, B. (2010). *Critical Global Perspectives: Rethinking Knowledge about Global Societies*. USA: Information Age Publishing.

Teekens, H. (2000). Teaching and learning in the international classroom. In P. Crowther, M. Joris, M. Otten, B. Nilsson, H. Teekens and B. Wächter, *Internationalisation at home: a position paper*. Amsterdam: EAIE.

Thornton, M. (2009). Academic un-freedom in the new knowledge economy. In A. Brew and L. Lucas (Eds.) *Academic Research and Researchers* (pp. 19–35). Maidenhead McGraw Hill: Open University Press.

Trahar, S. (2011). *Developing cultural capability in international higher education: a narrative enquiry*. Oxford: Routledge.

Trouillot, M.R. (2003). *Global transformations: anthropology and the modern world*. Basingstoke: Palgrave Macmillan.

Van Damme, D. (2001). Quality issues in the internationalisation of higher education. *Higher Education, 41*(4), 415–441.

Vandermensbrugghe, J. (2004) The Unbearable Vagueness of Critical Thinking in the Context of the Anglo-Saxonisation of Education. *International Education Journal, 5*(3), 417–422.

Wai Lo, W.Y. (2009). Reflections on internationalisation of higher education in Taiwan: perspectives and prospects. *Higher Education, 58*(6), 733–745.

Zhong, G. (2010). Education for a global era: reflections of an Asian teacher education faculty. In B. Subedi (Ed). *Critical Global Perspectives: Rethinking Knowledge about Global Societies* (pp. 161–181). USA: Information Age Publishing.

A narrative of unexpected cultural contribution: A critical cosmopolitan approach to global cultural politics and internationalation

7

Adrian Holliday

In this chapter I argue that where the internationalisation of higher education takes place within a Western context it involves a particular cultural global politics which is acted out in everyday, academic and institutional domains. Despite stated intentions to be sensitive and inclusive, this politics creates a deeply rooted preoccupation with defining and reducing an imagined foreign Other which stands in the way of appreciating the contribution of foreign students. I therefore consider what we need to understand to overcome this barrier.

Multiculturalism and Cultural Prejudice

Multiculturalism is a good place to begin because, in its liberal form, it represents a recent Western attempt to develop policies to appreciate cultural diversity through its artefacts, festivals, ceremonies, dress, food and customs. It has however been widely criticised for being a patronising, commodified, ritualised, boutique celebration of difference which has been far from faithful to the complexity of lived cultural experience (e.g. Delanty, Wodak & Jones, 2008a; Kubota, 2004, p. 5; Kumaravadivelu, 2007, p. 109). Liberal multiculturalism has also been criticised for harbouring neo-racism, where race is rationalised, hidden and denied under the 'nice' heading of culture (Delanty, Wodak & Jones, 2008b, p. 1; Hall, 1991a, p. 55; Spears,

1999). Indeed, the sheer enthusiasm of engaging with difference can lead to an exaggeration of stereotypes (Ryan & Louie, 2007, p. 407).

The uncomfortable knowledge that a well-wishing desire to understand difference can hide an almost unconscious positioning, or Othering, of foreign students as culturally deficient was evident in my own qualitative study of a language immersion programme for Hong Kong Chinese students in a UK university (Holliday, 2005, pp. 37, 94–113). My research aim was to critique the stereotype that the students' lack of inclination to speak in class was due to a cultural inability. However, in the process I was shocked to find that I was implicated in creating the stereotype, which I began to understand was therefore deeper in my society's world view than I had imagined. While no single piece of data was sufficient to make the point within the complex thick description that emerged, the following extract provides a degree of illustration:

> They had been to the Tate Modern Gallery in London on an excursion organized by the programme. I remember that the supervising tutor [A] had reported that none of the students had wanted to spend much time at the gallery and had seemed mostly interested in the souvenir shop.
>
> However, in the tutorial two of the students enthusiastically showed me postcards of paintings they had bought. I was impressed at the degree of sophistication with which they explained how the abstract paintings they had chosen, which they had also seen in the gallery, reminded them of images of city streets in Hong Kong, which they also linked to their knowledge of expressionism. (Holliday, 2005, p. 106)

At one level tutor A is simply annoyed that the students did not spend more time looking at paintings. At another level, the description implies that he is applying the common stereotype of East

Asian culture;, that the buying of presents, presumably for family and friends, represents a collectivist loyalty to group (e.g. Triandis, 2004, pp. x–xi) which takes up valuable time and is in conflict with the autonomy required to take full pedagogic advantage of the visit to the gallery. I then critique his use of the stereotype when I observe that the buying of presents was not in conflict with learning from the visit at all. On the contrary, they had bought postcards of expressionist paintings which demonstrated a high degree of engagement with the gallery.

There is however a still deeper interpretation, which I can validate through a discovered knowledge of my own thinking. I find myself being impressed and surprised at the Hong Kong students' knowledge of expressionist art, as though it is unexpected. I find myself thinking, in an unguarded moment, that this knowledge of 'Western' art is out of character with Chinese culture, and that the students must therefore be 'Westernised'. This is a particularly patronising aspect of cultural Othering – that a certain type of perceived 'sophisticated' knowledge and interest can only be gained outside the 'culture' in question. This is not a chauvinistic researcher discovering his own prejudices; it is an insider understanding of a sustained social phenomenon which can be further made sense of by looking at opposing social theories.

The theory which underpins this cultural prejudice derives from a structural-functional picture of society in which all behaviour and values can be predicted and explained by the structures of the national culture which contain them. Structural-functionalism can be traced back to the sociology of Emile Durkheim (e.g. 1964, first published in 1893) and is found in the currently influential work of Hofstede (e.g. 2003). It contributes to an essentialist view of culture, where individuals are defined almost entirely in terms of national cultural characteristics. The analysis of behaviour is positivist because it begins with established theories (i.e. collectivism) and then looks for confirmation of them.

Critical Cosmopolitanism

An alternative view of the Hong Kong students and their British tutors derives from the social action theory of Max Weber (e.g. 1964, first published in 1922). This picture of society gives individuals the ability to dialogue with social structures which influence but do not confine them. Individuals therefore have social abilities which can stand in resistance to or outside the cultural influences of nation.

An extension of this idea of negotiating culture comes from critical cosmopolitan argument (i) that cultural boundaries are blurred (e.g. Grande, 2006), imagined and constructed through political positioning within an unequal world (Hall, 1991b, 1991a; Hannerz, 1991);, (ii) that the West's notions of equal rights, universalism, humanism, and democracy do not extend beyond its borders (Delanty, et al., 2008b, p. 9; Kamali, 2008, p. 301);, and (iii) that the Western, Centre construction of culture defines the Periphery and hides its true cultural nature (Bhabha, 1994, pp. xiv–xvi). Hannerz (1991) defines the relationship between Centre and Periphery as one of imposing and taking meaning within an unequal global order. It therefore becomes apparent that structural-functionalism is politically and ideologically motivated, and not the neutral application of science which it claims to be.

Understanding what is going on between the Hong Kong students and their British tutors therefore requires making sense of the Western condition which underpins the perceptions of the tutors. This resonates with recent thinking in the internationalisation project, that it is not the foreign students who are the problem but the way in which we look at them (Robson, 2008). The break from essentialist thinking requires an appreciation that the Hong Kong students bringing postcards of expressionist paintings to the tutorial is not due to a 'Westernising' influence, but to an indigenous, cosmopolitan modernity which is unrecognised and Peripherised by the Centre-Western definition of who they are. Even if the students were buying presents for their families and friends at the expense of spending time looking at paintings, any suggestion that this behaviour is their defining characteristic, out of all the things that must have been going on during the visit to the gallery, is revealed as Othering. A further critical analysis of my description of the event tells me that I even intended the term 'souvenir shop' to imply 'unsophisticated', which the shops at the Tate Modern are certainly not, thus further denigrating the students' behaviour.

Neo-essentialism

There is a growing criticism of essentialism, especially with regard to Chinese students, in the internationalisation literature (e.g. Grimshaw, 2010a; Ryan & Louie, 2007). However, intercultural communication studies continues to sustain a strong neo-essentialist undercurrent, where writers decry essentialist categories and then to move on to use them (Holliday, 2011, p. 7, citing Ellis & Moaz, Gudykunst et al., Jandt, M-S Kim, Y Y Kim, Philipsen et al, Scollon & Scollon, Spencer-Oatey & Xing, and Triandis as examples). It is argued that this recidivism is driven by the need in the academy to build on established theory (Moon, 2008, p. 15; Shuter, 2008, p. 38), as well as by the inherent duality in the commodified celebration of difference in liberal multiculturalism described above.

This duality, where a surface tolerance hides a deeper essentialism, has been observed among home university students. While they state an appreciation of the value of engaging with diversity, by 'simply "dealing with it"' they are in danger of setting up 'an unequal dialogue that has the unintended consequence of marginalising particular groups and reinforcing stereotypes' (Caruana & Spurling, 2006, p. 8).

While these students claim to reject stereotyping, their fear of labelling leads to a deeper form of Othering whereby foreign students are referred to as indiscriminate members of groups rather than as individuals; and their common reference to 'language problems' becomes a euphemism for a less comfortable set of differences in behaviour and values (Harrison & Peacock, 2009, pp. 133, 136). The duality also exists where official institutional discourses of inclusion are not realized in the small detail of everyday implementation (Leask, 2009; Trahar, 2009, p. 143).

Claiming the World

Taking action to 'solve' cultural 'problems' may be at the core of the Western predicament. Instead, there is a bottom-up movement to claim cultural recognition coming from the Periphery (Fairclough, 2006, p. 121; Hall, 1991b, p. 34) which simply needs space and understanding. Examples of this can be seen in recent studies of the non-Western modernity implicit in grass-roots civil society in the Middle East which does not need the support of Western invasion. There are reports of how Afghan men broke away from expected masculine roles in support of their wives' and daughters' resistance to the Taliban régime (Rostami-Povey, 2007, p. 108). The existence of a long-standing tradition of radical resistance among Middle Eastern women, largely ignored or misunderstood by Western feminism, is catalogued in a number of places (e.g. Naghibi, 2007, p. xxiii; Osanloo, 2009, p. 201). Resonant with the Hong Kong students' appreciation of expressionism above is Honarbin-Holliday's (2008, p. 77) description of Iranian art students claiming Picasso and Matisse as their own heritage. Along with her sustained account of industrious working women who teach their brothers and fathers to break with tradition, demand access to football matches, run illegal life-drawing session at home, and drive a politicised café culture, there is description of indigenous university life with the seminars, interaction with tutors and project-based study. While the essentialist paradigm would consider this to be Westernised behaviour, Honarbin-Holliday insists that it is rooted in Iranian society and that women have inherited the modernity of their grandmothers.

Qing and the Seminar

The discussion so far has indicated that dominant perceptions of the behaviour of foreign students may seriously undervalue the cultural resources which they bring with them and can contribute to the internationalisation process. The following reconstructed ethnographic narrative, taken from Holliday (2011, p. 170), is based on the data collected from the Hong Kong students and their tutors in Canterbury and on conversations with other students from a range of national backgrounds concerning their experiences with academic life in Britain:

> Qing and her Chinese friend Tom were talking about their experience of British university seminars. Qing was anxious because she felt that everyone was always watching her wondering why she didn't talk. Tom said that she shouldn't worry so much because they weren't expected to speak because of their culture. Qing wasn't happy with this excuse – that 'East Asian' students had some sort of issue with 'face', and weren't prepared to make mistakes and be criticised in front of other students. Their lecturers also seemed to use this culture thing as a way of labelling people that they disapproved of. They were constructed as those 'problem students' who didn't speak and therefore were 'passive' and didn't think.
>
> She later had coffee with her Romanian friend, Lara, who had a completely different opinion. She said that she had read in her social science course before she came to Britain that face was a universal thing that different people

dealt with in different ways. She said that there was a particularly annoying student in one of her seminars who just wouldn't stop talking – and that that was his way of saving face. The irony was that he was also Chinese. Everyone knew that some people, from whatever society, covered up their deeper anxieties with extroverted behaviour.

Qing went back to Tom and said it was about time they took some action. She convinced him to help her to do some research about how to succeed in seminars. She had also done social science at university before she came to Britain and knew how to do this sort of research. They agreed to use their 'quiet' times to observe and note. They laughed because the British lecturers and the other students would never imagine what they were doing beneath the 'silence'.

After two weeks they met again and shared notes. It wasn't easy. Tom said that Qing was still clinging to stereotypes when she suggested that the British were just more assertive. Eventually they came up with the following types of student behaviour: (a) not attending the seminars at all, (b) trying to hide lack of preparation by talking off the point, avoiding eye contact, or not speaking, (c) posturing – sitting in certain places or in a certain way – to try and appear 'academic', (d) being quiet a lot of the time, but, when they did speak, showing they clearly had done the reading and knew what they were talking about, and responding to other students and also listening. There was quite a revelation here, and that there were some strategies that some of the quieter British students were using which both Qing and Tom could identify with.

Qing met Lara again and said that the research had been useful in helping to demystify some of the things that were going on in seminars and had shown a way through for a quiet student who was prepared to work hard. However, when she told Lara that she still felt very inadequate, she could see that Lara was immediately thinking this was because of her culture. She was therefore very careful to point out that if she was going to be one of those students who said little but clearly had done the work and knew what she was talking about, it was her knowledge of the language, not her culture, that got in the way. She said someone had to know a lot of English to transform what they had read into something to say about it in a short space of time – and also to actually break into a conversation that was dominated by noisy show-offs. Then she was shocked when Lara, who she thought had perfect English, said that she too struggled with all of these things, and she just hoped for a tutor who would shut up the so-called extroverts and help her find some space to speak. However, there were times when there were spaces for her to perform well – when she was asked questions directly, and when she was given the opportunity to give a short presentation.

Qing was very pleased when Lara offered to give her some tips on how to do this effectively. It was all to do with preparation. She was also pleased that she had used her Chinese university social science. She had always felt that the British, and her English teachers before she came to the university, had never shown any recognition that she might have any academic knowledge before she came to their classes. The research she had carried out with Tom, and the further conversations with Lara, even made her begin to believe that she had important skills to bring to the seminar issue, and that hard-working 'international' students like her might even begin to change the expectations of what was normal in British university seminars.

Analysis of cultural action

The following analysis applies a social action perspective to the narrative and employs four categories of cultural action (using cultural resources, global positioning and politics, statements about culture, and underlying universal cultural processes) developed in Holliday (2011, pp. 23, 130, 173). It focuses mainly on Qing's perceptions and seeks to demonstrate an interpretive image of cultural possibilities which are nevertheless rooted in research experience.

Regarding cultural resources, both Qing and Tom bring an ethos of hard work and collaboration associated with the expected Confucian background. However, they also bring a social science education which they do not feel is recognised by their British lecturers. This resonates with Holliday & Aboshiha's (2009, p. 11) report of British English language teachers saying that Japanese students have little access to knowledge of the world in their own education system.

Regarding global positioning, Qing's resistance against the stereotype of being 'quiet' and of being referred to as 'a culture' resonates with other Hong Kong students rejecting cultural stereotypes which they feel are associated with a colonial past, and also resisting the advice of their tutors and taking ownership of classroom space (Holliday, 2005, pp. 92, 98, citing Tong). This attitude of resistance may result in Othering British students and lecturers; but this needs to be seen within the context of students who feel themselves on the Periphery taking action against a Centre dominant discourse. Lara's position seems more ambivalent, as she aligns herself partly with a Centre and partly with a Periphery discourse in her response to Qing's ability as a researcher. This illustrates how cultural identity can be negotiated in different ways at different times depending on circumstance. International students in British universities can be as ambivalent about who they are as anyone else (Bourn, 2009, p. 24). There is also some resonance here with a study of Central and Eastern European

English language teachers re-aligning their cultural identities in different ways depending on their particular backgrounds when dealing with a profession dominated by teachers who have English as a first language (Petrić, 2009).

The strategic use of cultural resources and global positioning, and subsequent strategies of resistance, which may indeed include cultural Othering, also fall into the category of underlying universal processes. They transcend national cultural boundaries and provide the basis for all of us to operate as social actors in whatever circumstances we find ourselves. They enable and involve us in reading culture regardless of how strange it may appear. While the particular content may vary from place to place, we all equally take part in the business of constructing everyday rules for behaviour.

The statements people make about their culture are also part of this strategic process. They cannot be taken as evidence of what a culture is actually like, but of how people with particular cultural backgrounds respond to circumstances through the way in which they talk about these backgrounds. Hence, Qing saying that 'they' are not like the imposed stereotype, other students saying that they are collectivist, or Western people saying that they are individualist, are all strategic statements. Statements about culture are artefacts, outward expressions, or products of the politics and discourse of culture. They represent imagined cultural attributes, but may nevertheless influence action. For example, a social group may state that it has the best sporting achievements and believe this to be the case, while in actual fact it does not. Having the best sporting achievement is therefore in one sense imagined and unreal. It is nevertheless real in the minds of the group and will influence its behaviour. Individualism and collectivism are similarly imagined qualities that people believe about themselves and others. It can be argued that individualism, with its always positive characteristics of being able to organise, plan and promote self-determination, represents an idealised Western Self, while collectivism is also a Western construction which demonises the non-Western Other in its suggestion of inability in these areas (e.g. Kim, 2005, p. 108).

It is therefore superficial to say that evidence for East Asian students being collectivist is that they themselves claim it. What is more important is to understand the reasons for Tom's statement that it is more convenient to live with the imposed stereotype of 'silence' than to resist it. Chinese students conforming to an imposed stereotype is reported by Ryan and Louie (2007, p. 407). This can be interpreted as destructive self-Othering (Kumaravadivelu, 2006, p. 22) or as part of a long tradition of resistance by Periphery groups (Flam & Bauzamy, 2008; Sawyer & Jones, 2008, p. 245, citing Scott). Either way, Qing and Tom are engaging in underlying universal cultural processes. This theorising of such strategies among Chinese students could apply to anybody:

> They strategically employ cultural identities as a form of 'cultural capital' ... in order to build relationships, to justify their actions, to obtain leverage, or to generate content for academic assignments. Meanwhile, despite identifying themselves as reflexive and scientifically minded professionals, academic staff often accept uncritically the 'packaged realities' that are fed to them ... Cultural stereotypes function as tradable commodities. ... Students employ various strategies of self-presentation in order to project different selves, in different contexts, and for a range of purposes. (Grimshaw, 2010b, citing Bourdieu)

Unrecognised Contribution

This analysis of cultural action tells us several things about Qing's experience which are important for the internationalisation agenda. It is clear that she is not simply learning a new culture as a distant object in order to survive and get through her studies, but using universal cultural strategies creatively to capitalise on the cultural resources she brings with her to demystify and accommodate new and unfamiliar cultural practices. Because she has cultural abilities which are not incompatible within the broad domain of underlying universal cultural processes, her newcomer engagement has the potential to cause the cultural practice of the seminar to be expanded, enriched and to become more cosmopolitan. This potential for cultural change does not imply a change or drop in standards, but provides an opportunity for new interpretations – for example, an openness to a greater diversity of student behaviour. In this way, the very presence of students like Qing should expose home students and their tutors to more cosmopolitan realities and encourage them to engage with a broader set of cultural practices.

However, while there is some appreciation of what can be learnt from the working styles and attitudes brought by foreign students (Osmond & Roed, 2009, pp. 115, 120), the conservative forces of essentialism and the lack of recognition of Periphery cultural realities described throughout the chapter continue to get in the way of an appreciation of what students like Qing have to offer. A preoccupation with the collectivist stereotype hides and undervalues the possibility that foreign students can be as creative and ambivalent about their identities as anyone else. Hence, of all that Qing does and achieves, it may well be that only her silence is noticed. The common observation that foreign students like to stick with students from their own region (Osmond & Roed, 2009, p. 114), along with the experience of language problems and being a burden in group assignments (pp. 119–120), may lead other students and tutors to read too much into Qing's collaboration with Tom and draw attention away from their creative attempts to engage. The sophisticated use that Qing makes of the expanded experience of a diverse transnational community of students, as has been observed of other foreign students (Holliday, 2011, pp. 137–145; Montgomery & McDowell, 2009; Thom, 2009) is a valuable resource which may also remain unnoticed by home students and their tutors. Instead of an opportunity for expanding experience, diversity of behaviour is met with a fear of offending contravening political correctness and 'having to walk on "eggshells"' (Osmond & Roed, 2009, p. 118), which is sometimes shared by lecturers (Ryan & Viete, 2009, p. 307). The outcome is a widespread and well-catalogued feeling of isolation, rejection of friendship and exclusion from activities outside the classroom (Clifford, 2009, p. 173; Leask, 2009).

Gaining Critical Cultural Awareness

The solution to this lack of recognition would seem most obviously to lie in the domain of increasing cultural awareness on the part of home students and indeed their lecturers. There is a considerable amount of attention in the intercultural communication literature regarding intercultural awareness; and there is clearly some movement toward a more critical non-essentialist position (Spencer-Oatey & Franklin, 2009) which is largely to do with understanding unfamiliar cultural values (Byram, 2008, p. 162; Spencer-Oatey & Stadler, 2009) and to some degree appreciating Centre–Periphery cultural politics through critical pedagogy (Guilherme, 2002, pp. 92, 122). There is however an adherence to the notion of a national cultural line which keeps behaviours and values irrevocably apart and negates the possibility of underlying universal cultural processes which enable the cosmopolitan sharing of cultural expertise, thus maintaining a neo-essentialist position. The notion of a hybrid third space goes some way to allowing a cultural mixing, but still revolves around the cultural line which confines newcomers to a temporary, in-between 'limbo' (Kumaravadivelu, 2007, p. 5). For this reason I am cautious of a 'third space' or critical pedagogy (Ryan & Louie, 2007; Ryan & Viete, 2009) which encourage an 'us'–'them' attitude to cultural values or behaviour.

A critical cosmopolitan approach instead brings people from different cultural backgrounds together to pool their experience for the purpose of creating new action. Four principles are important here. The first is cultural difference as a resource rather than as a barrier. Wallace's (2003) work demonstrates how students from diverse backgrounds can work together to read cultural texts in which outsiders can see ideological and global positioning to which insiders are blind. This critical sharing enables a productive evaluation and 'contestation' of familiar cultural practices (Delanty, 2008, pp. 92–93).

The second principle is that the removal of an indelible cultural line depends on the possibility of a common language with which people can transcend cultural difference. An illuminating observation of where this may lie comes from a study of the attitudes of rural Chinese primary school children to their English language textbooks (Gong, 2010). While the students complain about the irrelevance of references of urban life, they present an 'inner world' which is essentially cosmopolitan; in which, like all of us, they 'express their ideas and emotions, tell stories of their life, share problems with friends' which 'parents do not understand'. There is thus a basis for a common cultural ground not only with urban students in China but also with students across the world. That such a shared world is there but unexpected is perhaps evidenced by study abroad volunteers starting out with a sensitivity about 'doing things wrong' and 'causing offence' and taking care to dress conservatively, then finding out that there was 'less of an issue than they had thought' (Jones, 2009, p. 86).

The third principle regards the need for a mutual belief that people from different backgrounds bring cultural experience which has value – that foreign students share a sufficient basis, through underlying universal cultural processes, to make a meaningful contribution to the cultural practices of home students. The apparent lack of such a belief is at the bottom of the issues discussed in this chapter. A fourth principle relates to personal space. Qing and Tom need the freedom to carry out their investigation and develop their strategies in their own time and on their own terms. Here it is important to be cautious of pedagogic solutions which exercise too much control of the learning process (Caruana & Spurling, 2006), where Japanese and Chinese students feel inhibited by too much control and surveillance in British university language classrooms, and where sometimes the traditional lecture at its best allows the privacy they need to be themselves (Holliday, 2005, pp. 63–84, 94) and the most rewarding experiences can be those which are uncontrolled and out of class (Lundgren, 2009, p. 147).

A Delicate Balance

Returning to my statement at the beginning of the chapter, where the internationalisation project is a Western intervention, caution must be exercised. There needs to be change to the way in which Western institutions, pedagogies and everyday perceptions construct the foreign. At the same time, 'change' is the speciality of the same Western condition. We are beginning to learn that our theories about the foreign, well-wishing though they may be, are more to do with our desire to construct than about the people they describe. This point is encapsulated by a Kuwaiti university student's request to her lecturer – to tell the people she was going to meet at a conference in the US – 'I think teachers need to understand that it's OK if they don't get everything about our culture and behaviour. ... We're just students you know; why have you got to understand us?' (Holliday, 2011, p. 102, citing Kamal). How can this immense statement of normality and independence be reconciled with the need for us, our students and our teachers to learn to understand? The point surely is, as my study of Hong Kong students indicates, that it is our own prejudices that we need to learn to understand.

References

Bhabha, H. (1994). *The location of culture*. London: Routledge.

Bourn, D. (2009). Students as global citizens. In E. Jones (Ed.), *Internationalisation and the student voice: higher education perspectives* (pp. 18–29). London: Routledge.

Byram, M. (2008). *From foreign language education to education for intercultural citizenship: essays and reflections*. Clevedon: Multilingual Matters.

Caruana, V., & Spurling, N. (2006). The internationalisation of UK higher education: a review of selected material. *The Higher Education Academy*. Retrieved February 5, 2010, from **http://www.heacademy.ac.uk/resources/detail/the_internationalis ation_of_uk_he**

Clifford, V. (2009). The internationalized curriculum. In E. Jones (Ed.), *Internationalisation and the student voice: higher education perspectives* (pp. 169–180). London: Routledge.

Delanty, G. (2008). Dilemmas of secularism: Europe, religion and the problem of pluralism. In G. Delanty, R. Wodak & P. Jones (Eds.), *Identity, belonging and migration* (pp. 78–97). Liverpool: Liverpool University Press.

Delanty, G., Wodak, R. & Jones, P. (Eds.). (2008a). *Identity, belonging and migration*. Liverpool: Liverpool University Press.

Delanty, G., Wodak, R. & Jones, P. (2008b). Introduction: migration, discrimination and belonging in Europe. In G. Delanty, R. Wodak & P. Jones (Eds.), *Identity, belonging and migration* (pp. 1–20). Liverpool: Liverpool University Press.

Durkheim, E. (1964). *The division of labour in society* (G. Simpson, Trans.). New York: Free Press.

Fairclough, N. (2006). *Language and globalization*. London: Routledge.

Flam, H. & Bauzamy, B. (2008). Symbolic violence. In G. Delanty, R. Wodak & P. Jones (Eds.), *Identity, belonging and migration* (pp. 221–240). Liverpool: Liverpool University Press.

Gong, Y. (2010, July). *A third approach to CLT in the Chinese EFL context.* Paper presented at the Cutting Edges Conference, Canterbury Christchurch University, Canterbury, UK.

Grande, E. (2006). Cosmopolitan political science. *British Journal of Sociology,* 57(1), 87–111.

Grimshaw, T. (2010a). Styling the occidental other: interculturality in Chinese university performances. *Language & Intercultural Communication, 10*(3), 243–258.

Grimshaw, T. (2010b, September). *Stereotypes as cultural capital: international students negotiating identities in British HE.* Paper presented at the British Association of Applied Linguistics Annual Conference: Applied Linguistics: Global and Local, University of Aberdeen, Scotland.

Guilherme, M. (2002). *Critical citizens for an intercultural world: foreign language education as cultural politics.* Clevedon: Multilingual Matters.

Hall, S. (1991a). Old and new identities, old and new ethnicities. In A. D. King (Ed.), *Culture, globalization and the world-system* (pp. 40–68). New York: Palgrave.

Hall, S. (1991b). The local and the global: globalization and ethnicity. In A. D. King (Ed.), *Culture, globalization and the world-system* (pp. 19–39). New York: Palgrave.

Hannerz, U. (1991). Scenarios of peripheral cultures. In A. D. King (Ed.), *Culture, globalization and the world-system* (pp. 107–128). New York: Palgrave.

Harrison, N. & Peacock, N. (2009). Interactions in the international classroom: the UK perspective. In E. Jones (Ed.), *Internationalisation and the student voice: higher education perspectives* (pp. 125–142). London: Routledge.

Hofstede, G. (2003). *Culture's consequences: comparing values, behaviours, institutions and organizations across cultures* (2nd ed.). London: Sage.

Holliday, A. R. (2005). *The struggle to teach English as an international language.* Oxford: Oxford University Press.

Holliday, A. R. (2011). *Intercultural communication and ideology*. London: Sage.

Holliday, A. R. & Aboshiha, P. A. (2009). The denial of ideology in perceptions of 'nonnative speaker' teachers. *TESOL Quarterly, 43*(4), 669–689.

Honarbin-Holliday, M. (2008). *Becoming visible in Iran: women in contemporary Iranian society*. London: I B Tauris.

Jones, E. (2009). 'Don't worry about the worries': transforming lives through international volunteering. In E. Jones (Ed.), *Internationalisation and the student voice: higher education perspectives* (pp. 83–97). London: Routledge.

Kamali, M. (2008). Conclusion: discrimination as a modern European legacy. In G. Delanty, R. Wodak & P. Jones (Eds.), *Identity, belonging and migration* (pp. 301–309). Liverpool: Liverpool University Press.

Kim, M-S. (2005). Culture-based conversational constraints theory. In W. B. Gudykunst (Ed.), *Theorizing about intercultural communication* (pp. 93–117). Thousand Oaks: Sage.

Kubota, R. (2004). Critical multiculturalism and second language education. In B. Norton & K. Toohey (Eds.), *Critical pedagogies and language learning* (pp. 30–52). Cambridge: Cambridge University Press.

Kumaravadivelu, B. (2006). Dangerous liaison: globalization, empire and TESOL. In J. Edge (Ed.), *(Re)locating TESOL in an age of empire: language and globalization* (pp. 1–26). London: Palgrave.

Kumaravadivelu, B. (2007). *Cultural globalization and language education*. Yale: Yale University Press.

Leask, B. (2009). 'Beside me is an empty chair' – the student experience of internationalisation. In E. Jones (Ed.), *Internationalisation and the student voice: higher education perspectives* (pp. 3–17). London: Routledge.

Lundgren, U. (2009). Intercultural teacher: a case study of a course In A. Feng, M. Byram & M. Fleming (Eds.), *Education and training: becoming interculturally competent* (pp. 132–151). Clevedon: Multilingual Matters.

Montgomery, C., & McDowell, L. (2009). Social networks and the international student experience: an international community of practice? *Journal of Studies in International Education, 13*(4), 455–466.

Moon, D. G. (2008). Concepts of 'culture': implications for intercultural communication research. In M. K. Asante, Y. Miike & J. Yin (Eds.), *The global intercultural communication reader* (pp. 11–26). New York: Routledge.

Naghibi, N. (2007). *Rethinking global sisterhood: Western feminism and Iran.* Minneapolis: University of Minnesota Press.

Osanloo, A. (2009). *The politics of women's rights in Iran.* Princeton: Princeton University Press.

Osmond, J. & Roed, J. (2009). Sometimes it means more work ... In E. Jones (Ed.), *Internationalisation and the student voice: higher education perspectives* (pp. 113–124). London: Routledge.

Petri , B. (2009). 'I thought I was an Easterner; it turns out I am a Westerner!': EIL migrant teacher identities. In F. Sharifian (Ed.), *English as an international language: perspectives and pedagogies* (pp. 135–150). Bristol: Multilingual matters.

Robson, S. (2008). *Internationalization: mapping the territory.* Paper presented at the ESRC Seminar, Rethinking the needs of international students: critical perspectives on the internationalisation of UK higher education institutions.

Rostami-Povey, E. (2007). *Afghan women: identity and invasion.* London: Zed Books.

Ryan, J. & Louie, K. (2007). False dichotomy? 'Western' and 'Confucian' concepts of scholarship and learning. *Educational Philosophy & Theory, 39*(4), 404–417.

Ryan, J. & Viete, R. (2009). Respectful interactions: learning with international students in the English-speaking academy. *Teaching in Higher Education, 14*(3), 303–314.

Sawyer, L. & Jones, P. (2008). Voices of migrants: solidarity and resistance. In G. Delanty, R. Wodak & P. Jones (Eds.), *Identity, belonging and migration* (pp. 241–260). Liverpool: Liverpool University Press.

Shuter, R. (2008). The centrality of culture. In M. K. Asante, Y. Miike & J. Yin (Eds.), *The global intercultural communication reader* (pp. 37–43). New York: Routledge.

Spears, A. K. (1999). Race and ideology: an introduction. In A. K. Spears (Ed.), *Race and ideology; language, symbolism, and popular culture* (pp. 11–58). Detroit: Wayne State University Press.

Spencer-Oatey, H. & Franklin, P. (2009). *Intercultural interaction: a multidisciplinary approach to intercultural communication*. London: Palgrave Macmillan.

Spencer-Oatey, H. & Stadler, S. (2009). The global people competency framework: competencies for effective intercultural interaction. *Warwick Occasional Papers in Applied Linguistics, 3*. Retrieved February 5, 2010, from **http://www.globalpeople.org.uk/, http://www.warwick.ac.uk/al/**

Thom, V. (2009). Mutual cultures. In E. Jones (Ed.), *Internationalisation and the student voice: higher education perspectives* (pp. 155–165). London: Routledge.

Trahar, S. (2009). Has everybody seen a swan?: stories from the internationalized classroom. In E. Jones (Ed.), *Internationalisation and the student voice: higher education perspectives* (pp. 143–154). London: Routledge.

Triandis, H. C. (2004). Forward. In D. Landis, J. M. Bennett & M. J. Bennett (Eds.), *Handbook of intercultural training* (3rd ed., pp. ix–xii). Thousand Oaks: Sage.

Wallace, C. (2003). *Critical reading in language education*. Basingstoke: Palgrave Macmillan.

Weber, M. (1964). *The theory of social and economic organization*. New York: The Free Press.

What is my PHD teaching me about the implications of using culturally sensitive concepts for educators and students?

8

Sally Davis

Abstract

This is a reflective paper of my PhD journey so far in attempting to shape and adopt my curricula to students' prospects and destinations in light of my PhD research, which focuses on how far the concept of rehabilitation as defined in the literature is culturally sensitive. I will briefly discuss the background to the study and the methodology; but the main focus will be on the results of the study so far and reflection on changes in my own attitude, the delivery of the programme that I teach and the implications for students and education more generally. My interest in this area has come from my experiences as a neurological rehabilitation nurse and a leader of an inter-disciplinary professional postgraduate programme on rehabilitation.

Introduction

Rehabilitation covers diverse areas, from drug/alcohol rehabilitation, and psychosocial rehabilitation, to physical rehabilitation. The focus of my study is on physical rehabilitation, which includes neurological, orthopaedic, spinal and cardiac conditions. Although termed physical rehabilitation, this also includes psychosocial aspects.

The literature defining rehabilitation is predominantly European (including the UK), or from the USA and Australia, and places an emphasis on concepts and values such as independence, autonomy, empowerment and individualism (Cardol, DeJong & Ward, 2002; Sinclair & Dickinson, 1998). It is these concepts which are promoted with regard to rehabilitation in the UK. There are approximately 12 UK postgraduate programmes that specialise in physical rehabilitation, and these are focused on musculoskeletal or neurological rehabilitation. The MSc in Rehabilitation programme, which I lead, focuses on concepts related to rehabilitation such as teamwork, goal planning, empowerment, independence and autonomy. This programme attracts mainly registered healthcare professionals including nurses, occupational therapists and physiotherapists from the UK and other countries. Before I came into contact with international students I had not considered whether rehabilitation 'happened' in countries like India, Pakistan and China. As I worked with our international students I became aware that these students had worked in rehabilitation wards and centres in India and Pakistan. Initially as we started to discuss concepts like autonomy, independence and goal planning students would say themselves that these concepts were not evident in their practice and they therefore felt that they were not engaged in rehabilitation. This made me reflect on whether the concepts of rehabilitation on which I was focusing in the UK MSc were culturally sensitive. This has implications for international students returning to their own countries and for home students when rehabilitating patients from different ethnic origins in the UK. If rehabilitation is about maximising an individual's quality of life, how can this be done effectively without taking into account the culture of that individual and the culture of their society?

Another 'stop and think' moment was in relation to the editing of, and writing for, a book entitled Rehabilitation: The Use of Theories and Models in Practice (Davis, 2006), which is now a key text for the MSc Rehabilitation. The key feature of this book is the use of the ICF

(International Classification of Functioning, Disability and Health, WHO, 2001) and other models in promoting inter-professional work in rehabilitation. The ICF can be described as a classification of the consequences of disease and identifies human functioning as operating at three different levels:

Level 1: the level of the body or body part: body functions, body structures;

Level 2: the whole person: activities of daily living, participation in life situations;

Level 3: the whole person in a social context taking into account environmental and personal factors.

It is this consideration of the person at different levels which makes it a valuable framework when considering rehabilitation, as it enables the team to consider all the factors that may affect the patient's rehabilitation journey. One of the contributors to the book, from Japan, challenged my views around individualism and collectivism and their effect on rehabilitation with his chapter on a cultural model for rehabilitation (this will be discussed later in this chapter). I began to realise that promoting individualism is not congruent with all cultures. Researching for and writing the book made me again reflect on whether rehabilitation is only about concepts like independence and empowerment, and how these fit into a collectivist culture. It also made me consider whether the ICF is a useful framework to consider the cultural sensitivity of rehabilitation, and this will be reflected upon further in this chapter.

In the literature 'culture' is described as a way of life (O'Hagan, 2001) and the way an individual views the world, being a member of a particular society (Helman, 1994). Patrinas and White (2001) identify a number of concepts that are relevant to understanding diverse cultures. These include family structures, communication, health practices and religious beliefs. Hofstede (1980) identifies a framework for measuring cultural traits across countries that uses individualism and collectivism as the main parameters. The emphasis on one's rights as an individual (individualism) versus the rights of the group over the individual (collectivism) has always appeared to me to be a key feature of rehabilitation, and one that is represented in the definitions of rehabilitation (Sinclair & Dickinson, 1998). Hofstede's work (1980) suggests that Western views tend to promote individualism, while in other countries collectivism is seen as the more important value (Triandis, 1995; Iwama, 2006a). However, such thinking has been challenged as a type of stereotyping:

> by representing people's individual behaviour as defined and restrained by the culture in which they live, agency is transferred away from the individual to the culture itself (Holliday, 2007, p. 3).

On reflection, I realised that I have been guilty of such stereotyping. Holliday's work (2007) highlighted for me the need to be aware of individuals' cultural values, and the implications of that for rehabilitation practice and the need to not categorise people into cultural types:

> culture is something that flows and shifts between us. It both binds us and separates us, but in different ways at different times and in different circumstances (Holliday, 2007, p. 4).

Saadah (2002) explored autonomy and participation in rehabilitation and concluded that accommodation and negotiation may be more appropriate values for rehabilitation within socio-cultural contexts that favour strong family relationships:

> There are few who would argue against autonomy,
> conceived as a basis for participation, to be the ultimate
> aim of rehabilitation. However, with the strong family
> relationships and different cultural backgrounds of the less
> developed countries, a `family centred deliberative process'
> based on accommodation and negotiation, is more
> acceptable, reliable and implementable in these
> communities (Saadah, 2002, p. 981).

There is no discussion of why accommodation and negotiation are more appropriate and how they differ from autonomy. There is a significant difference between these terms, with the key feature of autonomy being about being free from external control, while negotiation and accommodation are more about compromise, reaching an agreement. My first thought was that autonomy appears to fit more comfortably with the notion of individualism, but I then challenged myself as to whether that was the case. Thinking about it further and considering the lesson I have learnt from linking individualism and collectivism to different cultures, I realized that again it is about the individual and how they function within their culture. For some, having control will be conducive with their own values and beliefs: for others, having the opportunity to negotiate may be more appropriate. What perhaps is not appropriate is assuming that autonomy should be the aim of rehabilitation for all individuals.

Saadah (2002) recommends the need for a more appropriate structural framework for rehabilitation developed from a deeper understanding of various cultures and subcultures. At present such a structural framework does not exist. There is very little literature on the cultural sensitivity of rehabilitation. What there is focuses on the cultural competence of health care professionals rather than the meaning of rehabilitation in different cultures. Maybe this is because it is difficult to identify one meaning of rehabilitation that is culturally sensitive. Maybe trying to identify a definition of rehabilitation in itself is problematic, as it is then perhaps assumed that it is fixed. Maybe rehabilitation, in how it is defined, needs to be fluid where it responds to social change and conflicting demands, e.g. different demands from the patient and family and health care professionals. This may also relate to different expectations.

It was this thinking that led me to the focus of my PhD and the following research questions:

RQ 1: Is the concept of rehabilitation as identified in the literature and practised in Britain and elsewhere culturally sensitive?

RQ 2: What are the wider cultural factors that need to be considered to ensure that rehabilitation as defined in the literature and practised in Britain and elsewhere is culturally sensitive?

RQ 3: What are the implications of these factors for rehabilitation practice and education in Britain?

Methodology

Concept analysis is an approach that has been used extensively in Western nursing to identify concepts suitable for subsequent research (Penrod & Hupcey, 2005) and to develop nursing knowledge. Penrod and Hupcey (2005)

> assert that the power of concept analysis is to identify the existing theoretical strands that define a concept of interest and ultimately to tie and re-tie the conceptual knots to form a stronger, more coherent tapestry of theory. Theory (i.e. the tapestry) is strengthened as the individual strands (i.e. concepts) are clarified and developed (p. 404).

This analogy I feel relates well to rehabilitation, as rehabilitation is defined in the literature with key characteristics (theoretical strands) and related concepts. However, the current 'tapestry' of rehabilitation may not be coherent across cultures, with the commonly identified strands not being conducive to different cultures. It therefore seems appropriate to use concept analysis as the research approach in this study to explore the cultural sensitivity of 'rehabilitation' and to 're-tie the conceptual knots', or maybe to unravel the tapestry and avoid knots.

The approach to concept analysis developed by Morse (Morse, Hupcey, Mitcham & Lenz, 1996; Morse, 1995) has been adopted as the main research approach for this study. This approach uses techniques of qualitative enquiry such as secondary analysis of the literature, observation and interviews. The aim is to establish the maturity of a concept and then identify the stage of analysis which is appropriate for that stage. A mature concept has adequate definition and is utilised effectively in practice. Rehabilitation is a concept that appears to be well developed or mature, as there is a large amount of literature, including clinical evidence and instruments which measure aspects of rehabilitation. However, there is a marked lack of evidence on the use of the concept in different cultures. In terms of cultural sensitivity rehabilitation can be considered to be an immature concept with inadequate definitions. This then has implications for how the concept is being used in practice. In my supervision sessions we have discussed whether it matters if rehabilitation is a mature or immature concept. At this point in time I feel it does matter. Considering rehabilitation to be an immature concept in relation to cultural sensitivity, and following Morse's approach, enables insight into why the way rehabilitation is defined appears not to fit across cultural beliefs.

There are three phases to the study, which are related to the research questions (Table ten).

Phase One: Relates to research question 1	Concept analysis of the literature to explore the way rehabilitation is defined and discussed in the literature, identifying key attributes and related concepts.
Phase Two: Relates to research questions 1 and 2	Collection of data from patients, health care professionals, students and lecturers in Manipal University and Kasturba Hospital in India.
Phase Three: Relates to research questions 2 and 3	Focus on the wider cultural parameters and the implications for rehabilitation education and practice. Discuss the findings with rehabilitation practitioners and educators.

Table 10: Phases in the study

The first phase in the study has been to explore the way rehabilitation is defined and discussed in the literature, identifying key attributes and related concepts. (For more details of the literature search please email me).

In phase two I collected data from a University and Hospital in the Karnataka region of India over a period of three weeks. I felt that three weeks was a reasonable period for me to collect the data I needed and to be away from family and work. It was very much about achieving a balance. I collected data through: 13 individual interviews with patients and carers; 8 focus group interviews with occupational therapy, physiotherapy and nursing students, lecturers and practitioners; and observation on the wards. I chose India because most international students undertaking the MSc Rehabilitation that I lead are physiotherapists from India, and there is no literature from India on the meaning of rehabilitation. I also wanted the opportunity to see for myself what rehabilitation was like in one area of India (which I know is no way representative of India) and to be part of that culture, even though it was only for three weeks. However, as I was only focused on the data collection during that three weeks, I was able to become immersed in my study and the culture around me. The previous year I had visited different hospitals and universities in India, recommended by colleagues and Indian students. The hospital and university I chose are on the same campus and some of my students had completed their physiotherapy degrees there. Although English is the language spoken and written by the health care professionals, students and educators, it was not spoken by the majority of the patients and carers. Therefore I was allocated two postgraduate students as my guides, who translated for me when I was interviewing patients and carers.

In phase three, the last phase of the study, I hope to collaborate with the Centre for Health, Medicine and Society at Oxford Brookes University to gain a fuller understanding of the wider cultural determinants, and also to engage rehabilitation professionals and educators to discuss the findings from phases one and two.

Preliminary Results

This section will present the results so far from the literature review and the data in India. In order to identify whether a concept is mature Morse et al. (1996) advocate the use of evaluation criteria, i.e. concept definition, characteristics, preconditions and outcomes, and boundaries. This is my first step in identifying whether the concept of rehabilitation, in terms of cultural sensitivity, is a mature concept. NVivo 8 is being used to manage and query the data.

Literature review

As mentioned above, the literature on physical rehabilitation mostly focuses on a specific body function or treatment and mostly comes from the UK, Europe and the USA. There are a number of studies that focus on Community Based Rehabilitation (CBR) which is a focus for countries where there is a lesser Westernised influence. CBR is promoted by the World Health Organisation as a way forward for these countries. Participation is a key concept of CBR and also a key concept in the ICF (WHO 2001). The ICF is promoted in the literature not only as a way of classifying disability but also as a multi-disciplinary, holistic rehabilitation framework.

The cultural sensitivity of the concept of rehabilitation is only explicitly referred to in two sources: Saadah (2002) on autonomy, which I discussed earlier, and Iwama (2006a), an occupational therapist from Japan, who developed a culturally sensitive model specifically for occupational therapy practice in Japan. The Kawa Model (Iwama 2006b) uses the metaphor of nature to explain the Eastern perspective of harmony in life experience. River (Kawa) is used to represent an individual's life energy which flows through time and space, the model being compatible with Japanese cultural values and beliefs. Iwama (2006b) makes the point that the ICF may need alterations to meet individual diverse cultural conditions.

There are a number of concepts in the literature that are related to that of rehabilitation: client-centred care, autonomy, quality of life, and empowerment. It is not clear how transferable these are across cultures. Self-efficacy, self esteem, locus of control, and personality are all seen as predictors of quality of life in the rehabilitation literature. The definition by the World Health Organisation (2009) states:

> Rehabilitation of people with disabilities is a process aimed at enabling them to reach and maintain their optimal physical, sensory, intellectual, psychological and social functional levels. Rehabilitation provides disabled people with the tools they need to attain independence and self-determination (p. 1).

According to Morse et al. (1996) a concept needs to have a meaningful definition which enables it to be identifiable and recognisable by others. I will reflect on this in the next section.

Data from India

The data from India complements the literature review and this has enabled me to begin to identify the wider cultural determinants that have a bearing on rehabilitation practice. The preliminary findings identify that there is a difference between rural and urban areas in terms of expectations, facilities, and role of the family.

If we take rural India it is mostly giant families, but in urban India it becomes like that, they may be part of a giant family but they may be working in a different place so become a nuclear family. They may be working in a different state or city, so they stay separate, the others may not be able to come and stay with them. (Focus group interview: MSc nursing students)

This highlights how things are changing in India with more families being separated to work in the cities for the job opportunities and financial rewards. This view of difference between rural and urban areas relates to the previous discussion around collectivistic and individualistic values not correlating with countries. This difference between rural and urban areas came up quite a few times in the interviews, and appears to have an influence on how rehabilitation is seen and what is achievable. Throughout the interviews there was a key focus on families and financial restraints; maybe this was highlighted as I was collecting data in a rural area of India. It may not have been so prominent had I conducted the study in an urban area.

One of the key messages coming from the data is that rehabilitation was seen as a process in which motivation was important. This included motivation of the patient and their family. Linked to this was the view that rehabilitation must be meaningful; in other words, it should link to the patient's life and their goals. This was highlighted by students in the focus groups (FG) and also implied in the Indian patient interviews:

> For example if you have to get the patient to do strengthening exercise. Can't just tell them to just do the exercises. Tell him to fill up bag of sand or hold water bottle. Makes it more realistic. If it is something he already has he will do it. (FG2 : 8 physiotherapy students).

> For us in OT mostly treatment is adapted towards completing activities, we consider the patient's occupation and areas for maintaining previous life and activities of daily living and simulate them in our department and give those as part of the activity e.g. if a teacher comes in and there is some complaint of muscle strength weakness we would give him writing on the board, he would find that meaningful, that is the activity he has to do the whole day, that is his living so if he does that he will be motivated, then we will grade and adapt the environment. to facilitate all the possible deficits he has. That happens a lot in India. (FG1: 5 physiotherapy, 3 occupational therapy and 4 nursing students)

> And we have to consider their jobs, occupational problems which they may have sustained after hospital as well as family problems, maybe emotional. These factors have to be seen. How would the family member support them, the level of co-operation. That also matters. (FG3: 7 nursing students)

In an informal chat with a physiotherapist he made this observation:

> Rehabilitation is about motivation, this is very important …
> not all people will do the exercises, they just want to sit
> about and let their family do it for them particularly in rural
> areas … There is little evidence from India, we use Western
> literature … [it] doesn't take into account different cultures
> for example in India we use spoon not fork, use only left
> hand for toil, don't generally use Western style toilets.

On a similar theme an occupational therapist/lecturer made the
following distinction between Western and Indian society:

> So economic, literacy and social circumstances: that is
> where the differences in rehabilitation concepts between
> Western and Indian society are. (FG7: occupational therapy
> and physiotherapy lecturers/practitioners)

Both of these views highlight some of the differences between
Western and Indian cultures. There were no articles in the Indian
databases that defined rehabilitation. Definitions and aims of
rehabilitation in Indian text books were written by authors from the
USA and not specifically applied to an Indian context.

Discussion and Implications for My Own Teaching

This section will focus on the implications of the findings so far for
my own teaching, reflecting on the experience of collecting data in
India and the preliminary findings. My experience as a rehabilitation
professional and educator is fundamental to me and as such will
affect the way I am interpreting the data. Reflexivity (Forbes, 2008;
Adams, 2003; Finlay & Gough, 2003; Freshwater & Rolfe, 2001) is an
approach that recognises the impact of the researcher's subjectivity
and context has on all stages of the research project. In this study it

has been important that I reflect on my own attitudes and experience and the impact that has on the interpretation of the data. Reflexivity is a valuable tool which has helped me to do this. It offers a way of examining my own perspectives and position as a researcher and can open up unconscious motivations and implicit bias (Finlay & Gough, 2003) that I have which may have an effect on the approach I am using in my study. This has included my own reflections on my experiences and role and the implications of these in different contexts, for example cultural and institutional contexts. Finlay and Gough (2003) identify this as personal reflexivity. Reflexivity has been a key activity for me since the start of my PhD journey, and I have kept a reflexive journal of this journey which has included the data collection in India. As I am analysing the data I am also keeping reflective notes in NVivo.

Looking at reflections at the start of my journey I identified the following questions related to areas to be aware of:

> Which lens am I looking through e.g. cultural, professional, personal? What is my own definition of rehabilitation? How will it change/influence the study? To what extent is my view/bias influencing the literature search and interviews?

I have been aware of these questions as I have collected and analysed the data.

While in India, following my first two focus group interviews, I wrote:

> I asked questions prompted by the discussion. I used the opportunity to ask about the caste system, teamwork, concepts. Did I introduce new concepts? I guess my questions were guided by my own values and assumptions.

Although I did structure the interviews with some questions I found myself being guided by my own values and assumptions based on my experience and knowledge. I also felt I was being directive, and on hearing the transcript back it sounded like a structured interview rather than a focus group. I emailed a transcript of one of the interviews to another PhD student and colleague, who gave me some valuable feedback, and I also shared my anxieties with my supervisors. As a consequence, for subsequent focus groups, I set the scene, giving the participants more of an idea of what a focus group interview is like. I then asked them to give me an example of a patient who was successfully rehabilitated and a patient where rehabilitation was not so successful. I felt more confident with this approach, as reflected in my journal:

> I don't feel I was going into my lecturer role, I really felt I was facilitating and not directing the interview.

This experience made me even more aware of how I was seen in India and of the values and assumptions I was bringing with me. While in India I did at times feel isolated and unconfident:

> I felt overwhelmed by the interviews and the observation. Thinking back to Ann's (supervisor) comment of 'not losing confidence', I think I did do that a bit with the interviews in the first week.

It appears that I was overcompensating for feeling isolated and under-confident by becoming controlling. Although not particularly pleasant, I feel that this was perhaps a healthy feeling to go through, as it did make me reflect even more on what I was doing and how I was approaching people. It also made me email my colleague and supervisors for their views which, if I had felt everything was going well, I wouldn't have done; and then I would perhaps have not considered the influence my own subjectivity and context were having on the interviews.

One of the things that helped my confidence was to do with 'blending in'. Although I wore linen trousers and shirt in the first couple of days I felt very conspicuous. With the help of my guide I bought a couple of salwar suits (Indian trousers and tops), which were cooler, and made me feel more blended in with the environment. Although I know that I was still a 'strange white woman' and still conspicuous to others, I felt less obvious and people responded to me with a greeting and a smile.

At the end of the three weeks in India I was asked to give a lecture to the physiotherapy students about rehabilitation.

> As I went through the definitions I was able to relate their relevance to the interviews e.g. process, motivation, 'making it meaningful' health education. Also useful to consider locus of control as control has come up in the interviews generally in relation to motivation. Is locus of control a Western concept?

This reflects a change in the way I would normally talk about rehabilitation, which would focus on the definitions from the literature without considering the implications of them for different cultural values. The concept of locus of control relates to my previous discussion about becoming controlling, in that I am normally someone who has an internal locus of control and feels they have control. When not feeling in control, I feel I became more outwardly controlling.

When I returned to the UK after my visit to India I was aware of how my attitudes and feelings had changed towards what I felt about rehabilitation. My attitudes had also changed toward the international students, which was a surprise to me as I already took a key role in the School in terms of supporting international students. I felt I understood more the challenges the students faced coming to Britain for their studies. The international students (not only the Indian ones), knowing about my study, appeared to show more respect for me in wanting to find out for myself about a different culture.

In terms of rehabilitation, as I am analysing the literature I am asking questions of it which will help me develop my thinking. My experience of rehabilitation as a practitioner and educator is, I feel, helping me in asking these critical questions, e.g. 'Can rehabilitation be considered as a culture?' 'Does the move away from medical focused rehabilitation to more social rehabilitation make it more culturally conducive?'

As well as using these questions to further the analysis, I intend to use some of them and relevant subsequent questions to challenge the students' views in the rehabilitation theories module. I could do this in the work-book for the module and then pick it up in group work in the seminar. The advantage of this is that it will enable the students to look at the relevant articles critically in relation to the cultural sensitivity of the way rehabilitation is defined and described in the literature.

As a result of the preliminary review of the literature and collecting data in India, my teaching in the rehabilitation theories module has already changed in terms of discussing with the students the relevance of the definitions and aims identified in the literature for rehabilitation in different countries. I have stopped promoting autonomy as a main aim of rehabilitation, and have begun to talk about 'meaningful rehabilitation', that is, rehabilitation which means something to the individual and that relates to the individual's way of life and their goals. If rehabilitation is to be meaningful it then needs to be patient and family centred and culture centred. I realise that I assumed that autonomy was the main aim of rehabilitation, without considering the consequences of this for different cultures.

I am beginning to question whether the case studies I am using are culturally sensitive and whether they promote a globalised view of rehabilitation. Even though I use examples that represent different groups, I feel I am presenting them from my values base, which is about valuing the individual, which links more to individualism. Is this appropriate for all of them? In response to this experience I have started asking students to identify their own case study with the key information provided. It has been very interesting to see the names they use, and the factors they identify that are appropriate for that patient and their family: things that I would not have considered, because I am not seeing things in the same way. This has resulted in critical discussion about rehabilitation in different countries. I see this as framing things in a meaningful way for the students, and looking at the 'individual-in-the-family-in-the-culture' rather than the individual or the individual and their family.

I use some of the definitions identified in the literature review (as described earlier) in my teaching. On reflection I feel that these are not particularly recognisable to the international students, in that they can't relate them to the 'individual-in-the-family-in-the-culture'. The definitions seem to imply that the focus is on the person who is 'disabled'. There is no specific mention of the family or culture. It could be said that they reflect the individualistic view. I usually facilitate the students (in groups) to look at a number of definitions of rehabilitation, identify the key attributes, and then agree on a definition, which can be one of the existing ones or a new one. In future I will conduct this exercise in a different way. I will begin by asking the students to consider what the key cultural values (Patrinas & White, 2001) are that are generally used in their country in terms of: family structure; communication; health practices; and religious beliefs. I will then challenge them to look at definitions of rehabilitation through their own cultural values, with questions such as: What do the terms used mean, e.g. autonomy, and how do they relate to the main cultural values in your country/region? Are these definitions appropriate for use with your clients? Are they achievable? Finally I will ask them if they can identify a definition of rehabilitation which would fit in with their own cultural values.

I can see that there might be some difficulties with this group work with students not understanding what is required, and I will verbally help them with that. I will evaluate the group work and adapt it accordingly. The advantage I can see in doing an activity around definitions in this way is that the students are starting from the point of reflecting on their own countries and then using these values to look at the given definitions.

The rehabilitation theories module uses the ICF (WHO, 2006) as a framework to consider the themes of the module which are assessment, teamwork, goal planning, health promotion, quality of life and sexual wellbeing. Returning back to my original thoughts, I am now reflecting on how the ICF could be used to focus on different cultural interpretations of rehabilitation and the implications for practice. The ICF categories of participation (individual in a life situation), individual environment, societal environment and personal factors are already being used in the module to relate the themes to potential questions that could be added to the framework in terms of cultural sensitivity. These questions I am sure will come from further analysis of the data.

At the beginning of this journey I identified potential outcomes of the study. On reflection, it is encouraging to me that I am already progressing towards achieving them. These include the identification of cultural and contextual elements which have an influence on rehabilitation; the evaluation of educational materials for the MSc in

Rehabilitation; the identification of guidelines for the evaluation of any educational materials in relation to cultural sensitivity; the development of questions to challenge key groups e.g. World Health Organisation, International Society Rehabilitation Medicine, to consider their use of material, and definitions related to rehabilitation which are not transferable across cultures; as well as my own self-development and the enhancement of the cultural sensitivity of my own curriculum and teaching. Undertaking this PhD is enabling me to challenge my own teaching, but I have also begun to consider the implications of teaching any concepts that are not culturally sensitive.

Conclusion

Using personal reflexivity and a concept analysis approach has enabled me to think of the concept of rehabilitation in a structured way, and to move beyond accepting that the concept of rehabilitation is well developed in all areas. I have identified that rehabilitation, as taught in the UK, is being influenced by Western ideologies which are not always compatible with an individual's different cultural origins. It is for this reason that I commenced this journey, and I hope to identify strategies which can help rehabilitation educators and practitioners adopt a more culturally sensitive approach. Although the journey is not yet complete for me, my teaching and my attitudes towards rehabilitation as identified in the literature have already changed.

References

Adams, M. (2003). The reflexive self and culture: a critique. *British Journal of Sociology, 54*(2), 221–228.

Cardol M., DeJong BA. & Ward C. (2002). On autonomy and participation in rehabilitation. *Disability and Rehabilitation, 24*, 970–974.

Davis, S.M. (Ed). (2006). *Rehabilitation the use of theories and models in practice*. Oxford: Elsevier.

Finlay, L. & Gough, B. (2003). *Reflexivity: a practical guide for researchers in health and social sciences.* Oxford: Blackwell Science Ltd.

Forbes, J. (2008). Reflexivity in professional doctoral research. *Reflective Practice, 9*(4), 449–460.

Freshwater, D. & Rolfe, G. (2001). Critical reflexivity: A politically and ethically engaged research method for nursing. *Journal of Research in Nursing, 6*(1), 526–537.

Helman, C. (1994). *Culture, Health and illness.* Oxford: Butterworth-Heinmann.

Hofstede, G. (1980). *Culture's consequences: international difference in work-related values.* Beverly Hills, CA: Sage.

Holliday, A. (2007). Interrogating the concept of stereotypes in intercultural communication. In S. Hunston & D. Oakey (Eds.), *Introducing applied linguistics: concepts and skills.* London: Routledge.

Iwama, M.K. (2006a). *The Kawa model: culturally relevant occupational therapy.* Oxford: Churchill Livingstone.

Iwama, M.K. (2006b). The Kawa (river) model: Client centred rehabilitation in a cultural context. In S.M. Davis (Ed). *Rehabilitation the use of theories and models in practice.* Oxford: Elsevier.

Morse, J.M. (1995). Exploring the theoretical basis of nursing using advanced techniques of concept analysis. *Advances in Nursing Science, 17*(13), 31–46.

Morse, J.M., Hupcey J.E., Mitcham C. & Lenz E.R. (1996). Concept analysis in nursing research: a critical appraisal. *Scholarly Inquiry for Nursing Practice: An International Journal, 10*(3), 253–277.

O'Hagan, K. (2001).*Cultural competence in the caring professions.* London: Jessica Kingsley.

Patrinos, D.S., White, N. (2001). Culturally competent rehabilitation care. In J. B. Derstine & S.D. Hargrove (Eds). *Comprehensive Rehabilitation Nursing.* Philadelphia: WB Saunders Company.

Penrod, J. & Hupcey, J.E. (2005). Enhancing methodological clarity: principle-based concept analysis. *Journal of Advanced Nursing, 50*(4), 403–409.

Saddah, M.A. (2002). On autonomy and participation in rehabilitation. *Disability and Rehabilitation, 24*(18), 977–982.

Sinclair, A.& Dickinson, E. (1998). *Effective practice in rehabilitation: evidence from systematic reviews.* London: Kings Fund.

Triandis, H.C. (1995). *Individualism and collectivism.* Boulder: Westview Press.

World Health Organisation. (2001). *International Classification of Functioning, Disability and Health*: ICF. Geneva: World Health Organisation.

World Health Organisation. (2009). *Rehabilitation.* Geneva: World Health Organisation. Retrieved April 5, 2009 from **http://www.who.int/topics/rehabilitation/en.html**

Insights into hidden stories of crossing cultures: The CICIN poetry wall

9

Catherine Montgomery and Jane Spiro

Abstract

This chapter starts by considering the role that 'writing the self' has in qualitative enquiry, and makes a claim for the value of poetry and creative writing as a research resource. It shares examples of poetry selected by educators at a conference on 'global citizenship', invited to identify texts which represented for them the theme of 'crossing cultures'. The texts included those written by the delegates themselves, by students, or published works of others. These selections offer insights into participant experience of 'crossing cultures', and into their meanings and interpretations of the 'global citizen'. The chapter considers these insights, and the way learning can be enhanced and expressed through the medium of creative writing as distinct from more traditional academic discourse.

Introduction

One of the most striking arguments for pursuing qualitative research methodologies is that they can provide insights into the depths of human experience and search into the 'heart of matters'. Effective qualitative research can uncover 'truths' about people and their lives that can lead to a holistic conception of the lived experience (Furman,

2004). Qualitative researchers, by definition, have placed the subjectivity of the human condition at the heart of their enquiry, recognising that in the specificity of individual experience is the possibility for collective understanding: 'story may be told for personal reasons, but it has an impact on audiences that reverberates out in many directions at once' (Elbaz, 1992, p. 421). Qualitative research thus recognises personal experience as a viable form of 'data', and 'writing about the self' as a vehicle for learning (Richardson & Adams St Pierre, 2005). Reflective logs and diaries, autobiography, stories, poetry are all resources through which we can learn about ourselves and the human condition, and which involve forms of communication that go beyond academic discourse.

This chapter presents a collection of poetry brought together during the academic conference which generated some of the chapters in this book. It presents the poetry as part of the research processes involved in the conference. The aim of collecting poetry from participants of the conference, the 'poetry wall', was to provide an opportunity for them to 'write themselves' into the research process of the conference as they sought to understand the personal meanings associated with becoming a global citizen. The fifty conference participants were all practitioners in Higher Education contexts worldwide, including Australia, the US, Ireland and the UK. Their practice ranged across subject disciplines within the fields of health care, social sciences, education, arts and humanities; and they included both academic and support staff. All had, by virtue of their attendance at the conference, an interest in interpreting for their own practice and for their institution the notion of the 'global citizen'. Participants were invited to write and send in advance of the conference a piece of poetry or creative writing that expressed an element of their cross-cultural experience or their journey in becoming a global citizen. This could be something they had written themselves, something their students had written, or a piece of published work. This chapter presents some of this work and examines the idea of using poetry as a form of research in understanding the complex interrelationships involved in being a teacher or a learner in cross-cultural contexts. We used the form of poetry to 'access the more tacit layers of experience' (Burchell, 2010, p. 392) associated with teaching in a globalised context, developing an insight into personal conceptualisations of 'crossing cultures'.

Why should poetry be used in research?

In qualitative research there is often a question hanging over the relationship between subject and object, between the researcher, the researched and the resulting construction of 'data'. This is what Denzin (1997) saw as a crisis in representation in post-modern educational inquiry. Qualitative research topics are often viewed as 'riveting and research valuable' but reading qualitative research writing is seen as 'yes – boring' (Richardson & Adams St Pierre, 2005, p. 959). Even more importantly, as well as questioning the interest levels of traditional research reports, it is often thought that this sort of text does not capture the complexity and nuances of life experienced.

Poetry and creative writing more widely may have a role to play in addressing this issue, as it can open up for a wider range of audiences a 'deeper view of life in familiar contexts' (Clough, 2002, p. 8). Narratives, stories and poetry can allow the exploration of experiences that might not be possible through traditional representation, producing a different kind of knowledge and allowing the reader to 'feel into' the experience (Shipton, 2005). The use of poetry as 'data' enters the world of interpretive research, where accounts are seen as constructions of participants' understanding of their 'reality' rather than encoding any sort of 'truth'. The development of poetry or creative writing constitutes a form of understanding through which individuals make sense of themselves and their lives, and may also enable others who read it to rethink their own sense of self (ibid). If such idealistic claims sound too grand and unlikely to the reader, it may suffice to say that the in-depth and highly subjective data generated by poems or creative writing might help sensitise practitioners, teachers and students to the complex and diverse experiences of those with whom they work (Furman, 2004).

How can poetry and creative writing be used in research?

There has been a notable amount of research that has employed poetry and narrative – both as the research resource itself, from which rich data emerges; or as the medium through which research insights are conveyed. Bluett (2011), for example, writes a sequence of poems exploring her insight into the relationship between language skills. Spiro (2008) explains her experience of action research by constructing a story in the genre of myth. Here, the creative writing medium is chosen, because it offers a congruence with the core message of the research, in a way that a traditional research paper might not.

In this chapter we use poetry as a research resource yielding new insight into the way higher education educators perceive the 'crossing of cultures', and how they value this within their teaching. There are an increasing number of research projects which draw on creative writing in the same way. Jones (2010), for example, describes a project in which poetry is used as the means by which academics explore their identity in higher education. Teaching is a highly complex endeavour that draws on a range of different influences including teachers' experiences of being taught, the disciplinary and institutional culture as well as personal, cultural and intellectual dispositions learned through life experience (Jones, 2010; Clark Keefe, 2006). Because of this, poetry provides an opportunity to gain a different sort of insight into dimensions of the practitioner's experience, seeking to uncover the self as teacher, to discover ways of being a teacher and teachers' experience of the world as it relates to their experience of being in a cross-cultural context (Burchell, 2010; Feldman, 2002).

Previously, researcher-practitioners have used creative writing and poetry to interrogate both cross-cultural experience and practitioner experience of higher education. Trahar (2011) used stories, letters and narrative inquiry to illuminate the multilayered complexities of the lived experience of students and staff engaged in international higher education. Her book presents her own stories and letters to students in a form of autoethnography that illustrates how cross-cultural journeys can enable 'greater understanding between people from different contexts and academic traditions' (Trahar, 2011, p. vii). Burchell (2010) explored the more tacit dimensions of practitioner research experiences by using 'poetic expression' to build narratives of being involved in action research. Jones (2010) employed 'poetic transcription' in order to illustrate the range of influences that shape the way practitioners teach. This chapter aims to illustrate the cross-cultural experiences that could be said to have shaped teacher/learner understandings of themselves as 'global citizens'. In arriving at this understanding, the poetry readers/writers will have negotiated their own position amongst the various interpretations of 'global citizen'. On the one hand, the term could suggest commonality in a globalised world, focusing on what makes us the same, and even arriving at assumptions about 'sameness' (Cortazzi, 2000). On the other hand, the term could mean the capacity to cross intellectual and cultural boundaries, embracing and acknowledging diversity and variety, drawing on intercultural capacities such as those described by Byram (1997). In other words, is 'global citizenship' an invitation to conform, or to diversify? The poetry shared by participants provides some answers to how this concept is viewed and experienced. Here we use poetry in order to offer insights rather than build theory as such and to communicate something about teachers' (and learners') inner lives that have a bearing on their interaction in a higher education sector that has adopted 'internationalisation' as amongst its core contemporary attributes (Saunders, 2003). Here, the 'internationalised' university is interpreted equally as: a learning community which welcomes and includes participants of multiple countries, cultures and mother tongue; and a learning community in which intercultural competences are valued and developed for all participants, whether they are themselves 'travellers' in a new culture, or studying in their home context.

The CICIN Poetry Wall

The call for papers for the CICIN (Centre for International Curriculum Inquiry and Networking) conference included an invitation for staff to consider their own practice (or include the voice of their students) by offering a piece of creative writing written by themselves or their students. An underlying assumption of this request was that all participants were engaged in exploring the meaning and practice of 'global citizen', in order to make sense of it as a force for positive change. How this was interpreted remained a matter still for debate. The Poetry Wall was designed to look at the experiences and emotions which might not normally find expression within the context of a conference, but which are the hidden stories behind our professional acts and activities. It was also felt that these stories might be more immediately recognisable as something shared, universal, and emotionally engaging, through the medium of the poem.

The delegates were invited to:

- contribute to a poetry wall, sharing the stories, experiences and voices of your students, yourselves, or writers that have influenced you, describing the transition between cultures;
- write a short text – poetry, prose, or prose-poem – that captures the experience of 'crossing cultures' in any way you find interesting. It could be a text that has emerged from a classroom exercise, your own poem, a published poem that has inspired or influenced you.

The capacity of the poem to emotionally engage the reader is not self-evident. For several of the delegates, for example, a poem was a form they had shunned since school days. Comments included the fact that it was 'too easy' or conversely 'too difficult' and there was an assumption of a poem as linguistically challenging. For example, delegates had the view that poetic language was different from 'everyday' language, subverting received syntax, word functions and meanings. A second broad assumption was that the poem would not be relevant or relatable, that it would have nothing to say about real world experiences or emotions. Unlike curriculum change, it doesn't actually do anything.

In contrast to these arguments, we believed that an encounter with poetry that spoke directly about 'crossing cultures' might open new possibilities to these poetry sceptics. It would do so, firstly, because these poems would be direct offerings from other delegates sharing a common professional goal, so belonging in the same 'real world' context. Secondly, it draws on forms which are aesthetically pleasurable: rhyme and rhythm have qualities akin to music and metaphor generates surprise 'collision' between images and ideas. Thus, for example, a comparison between an inexperienced teacher in a class and a pack of wolves or a comparison between a breakthrough in language learning and cycling fast downhill activates empathy and imagination.

The poems which were submitted by participants were collected together and pinned up on poster boards during the conference so that they could be read during breaks. In addition to this, a session was scheduled into the conference programme where participants could come along, read their own poems or those of others, and listen to colleagues talk about the motivations behind writing. Both the poems pinned on the boards and the scheduled session received a lot of interest, and participants actively engaged with the idea. Some participants brought pieces of text and poetry that students had written, and another group of participants brought published poetry that they felt was significant. The notion of poetry itself was left open for participants to interpret as they wished. Some of the texts were identifiable as 'poetry' through line breaks, or features such as patterned rhymes or rhythm; other texts bore none of these features. What all had in common was simply the matter of length: the invitation to confine the text to one side of an A4 page.

We do not include the full collection of the texts here but a selection only. We chose to include the texts which had resonances with each other and which concentrated on the idea of crossing cultures. Only three teachers contributed original poetry of their own, and all of these are included here. There was a larger selection of learner poetry and so again we chose to include only those that focus on the idea of crossing cultures. We include a list of the published poems selected by participants. Once we had made our selection we looked for prominent themes across and within the poetry, and some of these are presented in the discussion section of this chapter. However, the main aim of this chapter is to present the contextualised selected poetry to the reader, along with a claim that such activities can provide insights into a tacit dimension of international education, and that these insights can be of value in articulating and clarifying otherwise hidden aspects of teachers' and learners' experience.

The Poems: The Hidden Stories

As indicated above, three types of poetry were collected for the poetry wall. Firstly, there were original contributions from teachers, participants at the conference, three of which are presented below. The second group of poetry was written by students of participants at the conference and four of these are presented below. Three of these poems (1, 2 and 4) emerged from a 'Poetry in a Foreign Language' competition, run in 1998 and advertised through British Councils and language schools worldwide, inviting students to submit poetry that explored their language learning experience (Bates, 1998). Poem 3 emerged from a poetry and language workshop with English language learners in Plymouth, Devon, UK (Spiro, 2004). The third group of poems were chosen by participants at the conference as being influential in their thinking about global citizenship. For copyright reasons these published poems are simply listed and referenced rather than presented in full. The poems told a number of hidden stories which might not have emerged in other ways as the drivers, or manifestations, of a commitment to global citizenship. They are presented here without introductions, so that the reader can consider them before themes are drawn out in the discussion part of this chapter.

Teacher poetry

Poem 1: Crossing by Emma Dawson

> They wouldn't let me in at first.
> Standing there, passport in hand, explaining why I needed to cross.
> It wasn't far – just a bridge. I could walk it – but I'd get shot.
> Five hours of forms, waiting, tea, copious staring and a conversation with a Kurdish (American) Private.
> He was there to protect his country he said, something he could only do in American khakis he said, and at the end of it all, he had an American home 'some place' he said .....
> But it was Summer 2005 and it was the Turkish-Iraqi border – it was to be expected.
>
> As I'm driven across 'the bridge' I hear the azaan announcing the drawing in of the day.
> I'm welcomed at the crossing point: 'the other side'.

My tired, sweaty, malleable passport receives its stamp
easily.
I walk on Iraqi soil, I get into the car. I look through the
cracked windscreen and the Iraqi landscape is thrown into
fragmented, confusing directions;
I'm left thinking, what is this Iraq?
and where do we go from here?

Poem 2: Return to the Fatherland by Jane Spiro

I first heard my nursery language
on some freezing platform
with dockland choking up a sunless dawn
clumps of consonants
grated together
like the crackling gossip of family teas

this they tell me
is the land where the sepia maiden
grew from girl to grandmother
and boys with soil black tresses
in velvet pants for the photographer
grew into leather satchels
and the long walk to school

if it is here
the place of mystic connections
if these are my roots
then I am no more than
the bird chained to its branch
the gallows with one leg on earth
the other blown to hell

we never rooted here, but
blew like pollen
dropping roots
where the wind ended
not where it began
not where the pistol shook out its seeds
one heavy summer

not in the place of invented pasts
of cartoon uncles in prayer shawls
or singing grandmas with candles
and chicken soup

but starting again
where we fell
where the double boots for deep frost
and prayer books were unpacked
where the cheese cake baked
again

I am not of this place
where I hear from dockland workers
 and drunken boys
the language of my grandfather's first prayers
and his last

(Published North Stone Review no. 12 1995, Minneapolis USA;
Broadcast West Country TV June 1997.)

Poem 3: Diaspora (for Ellie) by Catherine Montgomery

My daughter's face can span two continents
Her Celtic looks jewelled by Byzantine eyes
Chameleon smile, two cultures are content
Each country claims her proudly as its prize.
She knows she came from deep desire to roam
From ancient North through Anatolian plain
But wandering simply strengthened need for home
And parting all that kept her parents sane.
The years have drawn a veil on pain and loss
Entente and friendship change what once was tense
Breathtaking grace now builds the bridge across
She is the gift that means it all makes sense.
        While she can hold two countries in one hand
        There's no such thing as strange or hostile land.

Learner poetry

Poem 1: The White Room by Irene Soriano Florez, Spain

> I am now feeling
> Like a lost camel
> In the Sahara Desert.
> I am very young
> And I've got a lot of things
> To learn.
>
> Sometimes
> I think:
> I don't know anything
> I should go to my house
> And begin to study.
> But, then, I think
> Why? A lot of the time
> Knowledge flies after studying.
> Will I fly with English
> Out of this white room?

Poem 2: Wolves by Jim Scrivener, Hungary

> She taught as if she was stepping
> Over snakes she couldn't see; as if
>
> She stood alone, in a clearing, in a
> Forest, on a moonless night, knowing
>
> For certain (though not from howls
> Or snorted breath or from the soft
>
> Pawing of the earth) that all
> Around her, circled, waiting, eyes focussed
>
> Coldly, greenly, hidden
> Among the trees, the wolves
>
> Were massing,

Poem 3: Untitled by Miranda Lozidou, Greece

> I used to be shy
> But now I am not
> I used to be disloyal
> But now I've changed
> I used to not know myself
> But now I know who I am
> I used to dislike poetry
> But now I've become a poet

Poem 4: Learning a language by Olivia McMahon, Scotland

It's like doing a jigsaw puzzle
Of a million pieces
With a picture that keeps changing.
It's like getting lost in a foreign city
Without a map.
It's like playing tennis without a ball,
Like being an ant in a field of grasshoppers.
It's being an acrobat with a broken leg,
An actor without a script,
A carpenter without a saw,
A storyteller without a middle or an end.

But then gradually
It's like being out in the early morning
With the mists falling.
It's like a chink of light under a door,
Like finding the glove you were looking for.
Catching the train you thought you were going to miss,
Getting an unlooked-for present,
Exchanging a smile

And then one day it's like riding a bicycle
Very fast downhill.

Published poetry

Selection 1: Estrangement and belonging

Exile by Sophia de Mello Breyner (translated from the Portuguese by Richard Zenith)

The city that I have loved by Anna Akhmatova (translated from the Russian by Richard McKane)

The Emigree by Carol Rumens

Selection 2: Language

My Faithful Mother Tongue by Czeslaw Milosz (translated by the poet and Robert Hass)

The Language Issue by Nuala Ni' Dhomhnail (translated from the Irish by Paul Muldoon)

Selection 3: 'Culture'

English girl eats her first mango by John Agard

Discussion

The three poems written by teachers share common experiences of being and becoming a global citizen. All three poems tell of past life experiences in other cultures which may in part have led the teachers to be involved in international education. Cross-cultural heritages, relationships across cultures and travelling are strong themes in these poems and may resound with readers of this book who are also teachers in international contexts. The three poems present the story of crossing the border into Iraq as a war zone in 2005; portraits of children with a double cultural heritage embracing both parts of their background, one returning to Turkey, another visiting Poland, her father's country, for the first time. There are also complexities and contrasts across the poems with feelings of disjuncture from an Iraqi and Polish context in the first and second poems and experience of connection across cultures, with the child in Turkey as the bridge, that makes sense of past cross-cultural experiences. The metaphor of seeing the world through a cracked windscreen in Iraq and the image of the child standing in transit on a cold station platform in Poland are both powerful ways of communicating these teachers' experiences of crossing cultures. These are stories that reflect back to earlier or childhood experience that have remained with the teachers and appeared relevant to their sense of themselves within professional practice in international education.

The four poems written by learners present experiences of alienation and transformation as a result of crossing cultures, not only national cultures but crossing into professional cultures as a practising teacher. In the first poem the experience of coming to live and learn in a new culture is like being in a white room where there appears to be no contextual or cultural clues. The learner fears losing her sense of self as easily as she forgets the new language she is meant to be acquiring. In the second poem the trainee teacher stands alone in the hostile and dark environment of the classroom where crossing into the cultural community of teaching requires her to brave the 'wolves'. The third poem is a simple yet powerful story of change and of the transformational nature of the learning experience including the learner's surprise at becoming a poet. Finally, the development in learning a language is represented by a series of changing metaphors that begin in the early stages of language learning with it resembling being lost without a map or doing a huge, confusing jigsaw. But as the pieces of the jigsaw come together the metaphors change and learning a language is like finding a lost glove or catching a train that you had expected to miss. As competence develops it becomes like riding a bicycle downhill. These are stories of moving from a state of alienation and disjuncture in what appears to be a blank, confusing and hostile environment towards experiencing the satisfaction and personal change associated with developing intercultural and linguistic competence and the transformation inherent in learning about oneself.

The published poetry chosen by participants also revealed conceptualisations of what it means to be and become a global citizen. Strong and recurring themes in the poetry included feelings of estrangement and longing for home, and a sense that old and familiar places are seen in a new and different light after cross-cultural journeying, imposed or otherwise. Seeing the familiar as strange or as if for the first time also led in the selected poems to pride in one's culture, a clinging to one's mother tongue or to idealised images of one's city or country. These themes may have resonances with readers who have lived and worked in new cultural contexts.

So what did the poetry exchange actually do at the conference, in contrast to the papers on curriculum change, reflection and student voice? It appears to have changed the scepticism of some delegates that poems might indeed have something to offer, by demanding from the reader or listener a higher degree of emotional engagement. The experiences described became shared and alive, and were more deeply 'listened to' as a result. Thus, whilst much of the conference concerned the ways we wished to change our learners, this particular session, and the Poetry Wall itself, considered ways in which the delegates themselves might change or have changed, through the testimonies of others.

Conclusion

Using poetry as a type of inquiry underlines the significance of the personal. In this sense the 'data' is not presented as objective but in contrast in foregrounding the highly personal it shows how we are making meaning and sense of our personal and professional lives

(Jones, 2010). The poetry presented in this chapter has provided a different perspective on the lives of teachers and learners and highlighted the resonances in their experiences of crossing cultures. This can serve to recast roles of teachers and students into 'people-peers and colleagues' (Jones, 2010, p. 604).

The themes that have emerged from the poetry presented at the poetry wall have echoes with many of the issues that are raised elsewhere in this book. In particular the sense that the journey towards global citizenship is troublesome and challenging but personally and professionally transformative is prominent in this poetry and in other chapters of the book. The poetry has underlined the relevance and influential nature of the social and cultural experiences of teachers and learners, and how their pasts are relevant to their learning in the present. Perhaps it has emphasised that developing global citizenship in international higher education engages our 'whole' selves, our past experiences and our culture; and in so doing draws on this deeper engagement as a means to improve our teaching and learning.

Ben Okri notes in a poem chosen as part of the poetry wall:

'One way or another we are living the stories
planted in us early or along the way'
(Okri, 1997)

The aim of the poetry wall was to gain insights into the lived cross-cultural experience of teachers and learners in an internationalised education. As communication channels and media become more diverse and prominent as a result of globalisation and of technology, cultural and linguistic diversity also become more salient. People are now involved in many more divergent communities in contemporary life and the boundaries between these are becoming more blurred, including relationships between work teams, professional groups, voluntary organisations, neighbourhood groups and social groups; and these may be local and physically co-located or dispersed, virtual and global (Cope & Kalantzis, 2000). As communities become more interconnected, cross-cultural encounters become more commonplace, and the need to understand these as part of our life worlds becomes more acute.

References

Bates, M. (Ed.) (1998). *Poetry as a Foreign Language*. Edinburgh: White Adder Press.

Bluett, J. (2011). *The Distracted Globe*. ESRC Poetry Matters seminar. Nottingham: Nottingham Trent University unpublished PhD thesis.

Burchell, H. (2010). Poetic expression and poetic form in practitioner research. *Educational Action Research, 18*(3), 389–400.

Byram, M. (1997). *Teaching and Assessing Intercultural Communicative Competence*. Clevedon: Multilingual Matters.

Clark Keefe, K. (2006). Degrees of separation: An ourstory about working class and poverty-class academic identity. *Qualitative inquiry, 12*(6), 1180–1197.

Clough, P. (2002). *Narratives and Fictions in Educational Research*. Buckingham: Open University.

Cope, B. & Kalantzis, M. (Eds.) (2000). *Multiliteracies: literacy learning and the design of social futures*. London: Routledge.

Cortazzi, M. (2000). Languages, cultures, and cultures of learning in the global classroom. In W.K. Ho and C. Ward (Eds.), *Language in the Global Context: implications for the language classroom* (pp. 75–103). Singapore: SEAMEO RELC.

Denzin, N. (1997). *Interpretative Ethnography: Ethnographic Practices for the 21st Century*. London: Sage.

Elbaz, F. (1992). Hope, attentiveness and caring for difference: the moral voice in teaching. *Teaching and Teacher Education 8*, 421–432.

Feldman, A. (2002). Existential approaches to action research. *Educational Action Research, 10*(2), 233–251.

Furman, R. (2004). Using poetry and narrative as qualitative data: exploring a father's cancer though poetry. *Families, Systems and Health, 22*(2), 162–170.

Jones, A. (2010). Not some shrink-wrapped beautiful package: using poetry to explore academic life. *Teaching in Higher Education, 15*(5), 591–606.

Okri, B. (1997). *A way of being free.* London: Phoenix Paperbacks.

Richardson, L. & Adams St. Pierre, E. (2005). Writing: a method of inquiry. In N.K. Denzin & Y.S. Lincoln, (Eds). *The Sage Handbook of Qualitative Research* (Third Edition) (pp. 923–948). Thousand Oaks California: Sage.

Saunders, L. (2003). On flying, writing poetry and doing educational research. *British Educational Research Journal, 29*(2), 175–187.

Shipton, A. (2005). *Being and becoming a student in HE: an appreciation of an evolving sense of self.* Unpublished MPhil Thesis, College of York St John.

Spiro, J. (2004). *Creative Poetry Writing.* Oxford: Oxford University Press.

Spiro, J. (2008). *Learner and teacher as fellow travellers: story epilogue.* Bath: University of Bath. Retrieved March 2, 2011, from **www.actionresearch.net/living/janespiropdfphd/storyepilogue.pdf**

Trahar, S. (2011). *Developing intercultural capability in international higher education: a narrative inquiry.* Abingdon, Oxford: Routledge.

Published poetry

Agard, J. (1985). English girl eats her first mango. *New England Review and Bread Loaf Quarterly* 518. Retrieved March 2, 2011, from **http://www.jstor.org/pss/40375659**

Akhmatova, A. (2002) (trans. McKane, R). The city that I have loved. In N. Astley (ed.) *Staying Alive: real poems for unreal times.* Tarset, Northumberland: Bloodaxe, 334. Retrieved March 2, 2011 from **http://www.bloodaxebooks.com/**

Breyner, S. de Mello . (2002). Exile. In N. Astley (ed.) *Staying Alive: real poems for unreal times.* Tarset, Northumberland: Bloodaxe, 331. Retrieved March 2, 2011, from **http://www.bloodaxebooks.com/**

Milosz, C. (2002). My Faithful Mother Tongue. In N. Astley (ed.) *Staying Alive: real poems for unreal times.* Tarset, Northumberland: Bloodaxe, 336. Retrieved March 2, 2011, from **http://www.bloodaxebooks.com/**

Ni' Dhomhnail, N.(1990) (trans. Muldoon, P.). The Language Issue. *Pharaoh's Daughter.* County Meath Ireland: Gallery Press. Retrieved March 2, 2010, from **http://www.thepoem.co.uk/poems/dhomhnaill.htm**

Rumens, C. (1993). The Emigree. *Thinking of skins: new & selected poems.* Northumberland: Bloodaxe. Retrieved March 2, 2011, from **http://www.bloodaxebooks.com/**

Being and becoming a global citizen: Student perspectives on engagement, interdisciplinarity and boundary crossings

10

Dr. Catherine Montgomery, Mumba Chakulya,
John Paul Ndoumin and Claire Sedgwick

Abstract

This chapter focuses on student experience of voluntary activity in the community beyond the classroom, and examines the connections students make between this informal learning and their formal university studies. Three autoethnographic narratives of student experience are presented as examples of engagement with global citizenship, providing convincing first-hand accounts of how the informal curriculum can contribute to educating knowledgeable, multiliterate and socially adaptable future graduates. The chapter draws on the work of the New London Group (1996) and underlines the need for a wider perspective on university education in order that the informal curriculum can contribute to students making connections beyond the walls of the classroom, and thus developing multiliteracies that will enable them to live and work in complex contemporary environments and respond to the demands of a culturally and linguistically diverse globalised society.

Introduction and Background

The concept of the global citizen is complex and contested, as other chapters in this book testify. Some suggest that educating for global citizenship should be a common goal of educators and educational institutions (Shultz & Jorgensen, 2010), whilst others highlight the pitfalls of designing educational practices around the idea of global citizenship, which can be seen as a 'soft' concept (White & Openshaw, 2005). Despite this crisis of terminology two things are clear. Firstly, in university policies (such as teaching and learning strategies and corporate plans) there is increasing emphasis on social, political and environmental responsibilities and how these frame the purpose of higher education. Some of this emphasis is filtering though to the design of module and programme content (Bourne, McKenzie & Shiel, 2006), although this is by no means commonplace. Secondly, students are increasingly engaging both within and beyond the classroom in activity that acknowledges their role as a person and learner in an interconnected world.

Brian Simon underlined the crucial role of citizenship in education and argued that it should involve critical analysis and aim at transformation (cited in Brookes, 2005). This is congruent with the framing of global citizenship suggested in other chapters in this volume. Despite the potential that this sort of citizenship has to offer to the development of attributes such as 'critical analysis', valued by the formal university curriculum, voluntary or extra-curricular activity is not generally viewed as an important part of the student learning experience. Its framing as 'extra' to the curriculum indicates the way in which this sort of engagement is mostly construed.

This chapter examines student experience of voluntary activity in the community beyond the classroom, and considers the connections that students make between this informal learning activity and their university studies. Here student engagement in the informal curriculum of activity beyond the classroom is seen as contributing to their understanding of their academic discipline and its role in a globalised world, as well as to their own development as socially and ethically rounded graduates or global citizens. The chapter also suggests this underlines the need for a wider understanding of university education, and considers ways in which the informal learning experiences gained through volunteering can be reflected in learning at university. It is hoped that this student perspective may open a debate that will help us see 'what education can plausibly be and what new conceptions can, need and should be developed' (Kress, 2000, p. 138).

This chapter will be based around the ideas of the New London Group, who worked on a theoretical overview of the connections between the changing social environment facing students and teachers and a new approach to literacy pedagogies that they called 'multiliteracies' (The New London Group, 1996). More than a decade ago in 2000, Kress suggested a need for a 'new curriculum' that would be suitable for the future, with a shifting locus of site (where knowledge is delivered), time (when learning occurs), and authority (what counts as knowledge). He suggested that we need a new sort of education for the modern world which blurs the boundaries between curriculum and community (Kress, 2000, p. 141).

This chapter presents student perceptions in three case studies drawn from a purposive selection of student accounts of engagement with activity beyond the classroom. The three accounts are written by the students themselves and they illuminate the connections and associations that students are making between their active citizenship and what they learn at university. It is hoped that this chapter may suggest some ways forward in thinking differently about university learning and about the role of the university in educating globally aware, responsible graduates.

Multiliteracy and the work of the New London Group

The New London Group (including eminent linguists and educationalists Fairclough, Kress, Cope and Kalantzis), considered the influence of technology on literacy and meaning-making in learning contexts. In earlier twentieth century times the modes or genres that young people learned through were less diverse and relied mainly on written or oral 'texts'. The group felt that this was changing and that the 'emerging world of meaning-making would be more multi-modal... in which written, oral, visual, spatial, gestural and tactile modes of representation would be more closely intertwined.' (Kalantzis & Cope, 2010, p. xiii). As a result of this change in the way 'meanings' are made or represented in the worlds beyond schools, in work, in citizenship and personal life, the group suggested that new approaches were needed for literacy teaching and learning (Cope & Kalantzis, 2009).

In addition to addressing the concern of 'the multiplicity of communications channels and media' the group also saw the 'increasing salience of cultural and linguistic diversity' which is a result of this as a crucial factor in future learning contexts (The New London Group 1996, p. 60). The group argued that young people and learners are involved in many more divergent communities in contemporary life, including work teams, professional groups, voluntary organisations, neighbourhood groups and social groups; and these may be local and physically co-located or dispersed, virtual and global (Cope & Kalantzis, 2000). It is more common in a technologically enhanced world that individuals may belong to multiple life worlds made accessible to them by electronic communication and the internet. The increase in the variety and range of these groups means a much more salient and active interface with other social, linguistic and cultural groups. This increased immediacy of diversity and interconnectedness with global neighbours demands new sorts of literacy and wider sets of competences that the group called 'multiliteracies'. The group saw a need for change in ways of thinking about designing literacy and learning and presented 'the centrality of diversity... the significance of multimodality and the need for a more holistic approach to pedagogy' as crucial considerations (Cope & Kalantzis, 2009, p. 167).

The New London Group viewed multiliteracy as a development from earlier forms of pedagogy which taught skills and competence. Pedagogy for multiliterate graduates acknowledges the role of the social and of agency in learning and seeks to create a more productive, relevant, innovative and 'emancipatory' pedagogy (Cope & Kalantzis, 2009). This requires learning experiences that are powerful and transformative, developing a critical capacity where a learner interrogates the interests behind a meaning or action and their own processes of thinking (Kalantzis & Cope, 2005). This sort of process enables both a cultural self-knowledge and the furthering of disciplinary knowledge. In order to develop multiliterate graduates, learning needs to be multimodal, drawing on varied sources and types of information. A curriculum for multiliteracy would employ different modes of communicating learning and seek out different sources for learning.

The principles underpinning the work by the New London Group are of relevance to consideration of the influence of the informal curriculum on learning at university. The case studies included in this chapter demonstrate students engaging critically with their environment, making connections between their learning beyond the classroom and their perspectives on their subjects, and developing a broader portfolio of 'literacies' relevant to their professional and personal lives both within and beyond higher education.

Methodology

This paper presents three case studies which are part of a wider project, a multi-site case study exploring teaching, learning and assessment in an internationalised university context. This larger set of case studies is situated in the context of a five year research programme of a Centre for Excellence in Teaching and Learning (CETL), comprising both longitudinal data (for example, charting the development of student perceptions of intercultural communication in Design education over a three year period) and multi-disciplinary case studies that investigate student perceptions of intercultural interaction across different disciplines (for example, in Business, Design and Engineering) (Montgomery, 2009).

The three case studies focused on here were selected from contributions to a student conference held in March 2010 as part of the research project described above. 'Educating the global citizen' was the third in a series of student-led conferences examining student engagement with internationalisation. The conference focused in particular on the idea of the global citizen, asking how a university education might prepare graduates competent to live and work in a globalised society. There were student-led presentations that illustrated a wide range of voluntary and curriculum-based projects integrating an international element. It is from that set of presentations that the three student accounts included in this chapter were drawn.

Initially the three cases were selected for inclusion in a keynote speech to the 2010 CICIN (Centre for International Curriculum Inquiry and Networking) conference. Three students from a range of disciplinary and cultural backgrounds were selected (as a representative sample of the range of presentations at the conference) to accompany the author to present the keynote at the conference, speaking about the impact of their experiences of volunteering on their learning at university. It is acknowledged here that the students' involvement in the development of this material highlights it as a co-construction of their experiences, positioning them and the author as 'researchers as subjects' (Denzin & Lincoln, 2003). Their reflexive accounts are coloured but also enhanced by their positions inside the research itself.

By including these socially constructed narratives of experience, this chapter is drawing on the methodology of autoethnography and attempting to present complex pictures of lived experience. It is hoped that the accounts will reflect the flow of thoughts and meanings of the student experience and communicate them with some immediacy (ibid). Trahar notes that autoethnography is congruent and suitable as a means of exploring 'across cultures'. This approach to research, however, cannot be 'parcelled up into neat little chunks, each phase done and stored away' but represents a 'shifting, moving, interacting complexity' (Trahar, 2011, p. 38). Despite this, the discussion that follows the accounts will aim to draw out some of the salient issues raised by the student narratives. The accounts provide convincing first-hand accounts of how engagement with the informal curriculum can contribute to educating knowledgeable, multiliterate and socially adaptable future graduates.

The student accounts

Mumba Chakulya: making connections

My name is Mumba Chakulya and I am an International Student studying Law on a four year exempting Law Degree with the hope of one day practising as a solicitor at Law in England and Wales. The Law degree here is very different from my country of origin, Zambia, and at first I found the Law course to be very focused on particular aspects of the law and very academic and theoretical. The university idea of Law seemed to be traditional and had strong boundaries. After a few months on the course I got involved in working with an organisation called World Vision that has helped me to see my degree differently and has allowed me to explore different aspects of Law that I originally thought were out of my reach.

I have always had an innate interest in human rights and civil liberties and working for World Vision has helped me to develop my interest in human rights and see this as another part of my discipline. The main aim of World Vision is that it works to alleviate poverty and social injustice around the world. I have discovered that this sort of activity is closely bound up in the Law and has taught me about how Law interacts with ideas and communities in the real world.

I first heard about World Vision when I lived in Zambia. At the time, the charity was involved in a number of HIV/AIDS programs as the HIV/AIDS pandemic was at its peak in Zambia as well as Southern Africa as a whole. The second time I came across the charity was when I was in Leicester during Easter break and I randomly picked up a magazine and saw a World Vision advertisement that stated that the charity was looking for seven young people who would play the role of youth ambassadors for the charity all across the United Kingdom. The job was to last a year. I applied for the job and I was picked as one of the youth ambassadors representing young people in England.

Having worked with the charity for a year, I have been able to contribute a lot and learn a great deal about myself and about the nature of working in a Law context within the discipline of human rights. I also brought something different to the table in the sense that I am from Zambia and I know firsthand the effects that poverty and illiteracy can have on a community. I had seen it every day for years but I was one of a handful of the lucky few that lived a good life in Zambia.

Working with World Vision for a year was an amazing experience. The fact that I had the opportunity to engage in such inspiring projects prompted me to start a World Vision society at my own university. Over the year, this society has grown so much and has involved so many young people in campaigns that are life changing. It has given other students at my university a chance to see something of the discipline of Law in action, giving them a sighting of a different discipline to their own – as the young people who take part are from across the different schools of the university. It has also allowed young people at the university to be participants in activity that promotes change in communities beyond their own.

So far, the campaigns that the society has run have included a campaign to raise awareness of the fact that HIV/AIDS is a global issue worldwide; raising money for Jeevan Asha Healthy Highway, a project based in Jaipur, India, alleviating the exploitation of young girls commercially; taking part in a mobilisation rally leading up to the world's governmental summit; and fundraising to support solutions to the ongoing problem of sexual exploitation, discrimination and ill health being faced by the children of Chennai in South East India.

Since starting my work with World Vision I have chosen options on my degree that relate to my interests in human rights. I have expanded my international education from beyond what I saw as the narrow discipline of Law to a more interdisciplinary experience that has helped me see how it works in the wider society.

Needless to say, not every student is given the opportunity or is even aware of this path. Some learning experiences remain classroom-based and to my mind archaic. Sometimes learning seems to be based on what you are taught by your lecturers and your ability to reproduce that information onto paper. Students sometimes don't really challenge what they are taught and aren't really being given the practical experience of what they are learning. Universities need to start pushing for a wider curriculum that includes a broader view of learning and helps students to start expanding their knowledge beyond the confines of one single discipline.

John Paul Ndoumin: developing as a multi-literate graduate

I was able to become a student in the UK through the generosity of charity sponsorship in the Cameroon and also some support from my family. It has been eight years since I came from the Cameroon to the UK and since then I have learned such a wide range of things as a result of everything that has happened to me here. Life in Cameroon is very different from the UK but as a student I have had the chance to encounter a very wide variety of people who have been such an inspiration and who have taught me such different things.

The first and second year as an undergraduate student were not easy for me because my English language skills were poor and this made it difficult to interact with people and make friends. As time went on I got involved with the university language service and joined the university international student society committee as a representative for the Africa region. This was where it all started to look promising for me and I started to communicate during meetings, debates and conferences. I passed my Diploma in Modern Languages and I decided to put the skills I had gathered into the service of others and so contacted my academic tutor for advice on how to get involved with a voluntary organisation. She referred me to the North of England Refugee Service. I decided to give my time as a voluntary interpreter and translator from French into English and from some African dialects such as Bamileke, Lingala, Bassakou into English. I felt so proud to be able to put the skills I had learned into practice.

By now I was starting my final year of my BA in Contemporary Language Studies and I was asked by my module leader to choose between two options which are part of my degree programme: international trade, or a 'Students into Schools' module. I chose the latter, which involves final year students in schools helping to raise aspiration among young people. I did two weeks' teacher training during the module and linked it with voluntary action after the module. I came up with the idea of setting up an evening class in English at the local college to help asylum seekers, refugees and migrant workers to improve their language and gain an insight into the British way of life. There were a total of 28 people attending the class which covered areas such as family integration, job searching, grammar, vocabulary and pronunciation. At the end of every session I always made sure that everyone left with a short story about him or herself and what they planned to do once they were able to speak English. I was trying to raise aspiration amongst those who are less likely to integrate because of the language barrier. I always used myself as an example of someone who had poor language skills to start with but was now in a position to use my skills. Some of the people I taught are now working in the city and I see them from time to time.

Now I am working in a number of different settings. After finishing my degree in languages I did a Masters in Conference and Event Management and now I am working as a translator and interpreter for some agencies including Sky Sports and some Premiership Football Clubs and freelance as a conference coordinator. I translate from French, Italian and African dialects into English and have been involved in organising conferences at the Sage in Newcastle and at Northumbria University. My commitment to overcome the language barriers and get fully involved in UK society and learn about the host community has been strongly supported by the different sorts of social networks and groups I have got into. By getting involved in the voluntary sector I have developed a huge range of different sorts of skills that I don't think I would have done without involvement in such a lot of different groups and projects. My social networks and community work have been a vital and powerful factor in realising my career as an interpreter, translator and conference consultant. These factors also helped me to write about my experience and win the regional 2007 British Council international student 'Shine' award, which recognises students who have learned new skills, achieved personal ambitions, enjoyed new experiences and made a contribution to their institution.

If we are going to make university learning a memorable, enjoyable and important process and experience for all, I think it is crucial for students to be able to develop a very wide range of skills and abilities. These will come from being involved in a wide range of experiences that come from the classroom but extend beyond it, in the way that my experience has. Students may be future leaders of our generation, and they might learn this through interaction with varied communities and experience in different social settings.

Claire Sedgwick: crossing boundaries and borders

I am a final year English Literature student from the North of England, and during the last two years I have become involved in a project that enables refugees and asylum seekers to engage in creative writing. My account will look at the way a voluntary project that I led crossed boundaries between the formal curriculum I was learning at university and the informal learning beyond the university in the community. I used my knowledge as a student to help provide greater access for asylum seekers and refugees, a social group that has traditionally not had access to literature. Furthermore, my voluntary experience has fed back into my academic studies, supporting the development of my BA dissertation.

In January 2009, a writing group was set up by the North of England Refugee Service and the Literary and Philosophical Society in Newcastle. The aim was to provide refugees and asylum seekers with a space to share their experiences creatively in a safe environment, to make new friends and to improve literacy skills. Working with another volunteer who taught on the project, I became project leader and was able to make key decisions with the group and arrange funding from a youth volunteering organisation for an anthology of creative writing to be produced, celebrating the achievements of the first ten weeks of the project.

Writing group members selected the work they wished to be included, with each writer having an equal amount of work in the anthology. The selection of writing was then typeset and printed into a stapled booklet. The front and back cover were designed by group members, further emphasising the importance of the anthology as a product of the group's achievement. We organised a launch at the Literary and Philosophical society and guests were given copies of the anthology. The launch was a celebration of the first stage of the project, and also provided a useful way of promoting the project. As a result of the launch there was an increase in attendance at the group.

The project provided a way for me to apply my skills and experiences as an English Literature student to a community setting. I was particularly interested in the issue of access to literature, this interest being partly initiated by the fact that during my degree I had studied how the canon of English Literature had tended to privilege a dominant white middle-class experience. When looking for voluntary work, I wanted to do something which provided greater access to literature, as my academic work written for my degree had strongly criticised the way in which literature has marginalised certain groups in society. The refugee and asylum seeker community often have less access to literature, perhaps unaware of the opportunities available or unable to afford to attend events and courses because of low income. I felt that perhaps there was a gulf between the strong writing community that has evolved in Newcastle, and the low access to literature for refugees and asylum seekers.

Whilst my academic studies influenced the type of volunteering I chose to do, I think that my experiences volunteering also informed my academic study. When researching my dissertation, I chose to write about public poetry, with a particular emphasis on the role poetry plays in describing the experiences of the nation. Although not directly linked to the project (my dissertation reflected the formal understanding of literature and was about the poet laureate, rather than community writing), I used the opinions and ideas that I had formed whilst volunteering to help develop my argument. There was an interaction between the knowledge I had learnt through volunteering and through my degree, so that they informed each other. However, I was applying my practical experience volunteering into a theoretical argument for my dissertation, and did not receive academic credit for my project. Volunteering at my university is run from the students' union, and there was no input from academic staff. There is maintenance of a clear binary, where volunteering and other type of community engagement is seen as 'extra' to the work taught on the academic syllabus.

In order for the university to engage more in the local and in the case of engaging with refugee and asylum seekers the local-global community, these sorts of real-life community projects need to become integral to a student's education. Although English Literature is highly theoretical at times, the theories taught in the classroom can be understood more clearly when seen in relation to real projects. This would make the social use of an English Literature degree more clear, and would also reward those who actively attempt to apply their knowledge for a social benefit, creating a culture which encourages students to become more responsible and globally-aware citizens.

Discussion

The global citizen and making connections

The pedagogical model suggested by the New London Group stipulates that students need to feel a sense of belonging in relation to the content being learned, ways of knowing, and the learning community itself (Rennie, 2010). This has links with work that suggests that connections with students' lifeworlds are crucial to profound learning experiences (Beard, Clegg & Smith, 2007), and also with research that argues for 'authenticity' in learning (Montgomery, 2009; Gullikers, 2004). This sense of belonging incorporates students individual subjectivities and includes students' values, social orientations and world experiences in ways of learning and knowing (Rennie, 2010).

The accounts of student experience presented in this chapter demonstrate that students are seeing their disciplines in the context of an interconnected world with, for example, Mumba broadening her learning of Law to her active experience in Human Rights. Mumba's role as World Vision ambassador and civil lobbyist uses her developing understandings of the role of Law to contribute to the solving of complex modern problems, setting the formal curriculum into the context of an affective, civic and moral curriculum (Haigh,

2008). Mumba's story makes connections between her personal, academic and professional trajectories and makes a meaningful narrative that integrates her study of Law with her development as a responsible and ethical citizen.

Razbully and Bamber note that 'an increasingly interconnected and globalised world has necessitated a parallel interconnectivity within the curriculum' and students should be encouraged to 'explore, practise and critically evaluate the nature of the relationship between... the global dimension and opportunities for global citizenship' (2008, p. 1). Despite this, university education continues to miss opportunities to encourage this making of connections. Research has shown that both at college and university, messages within the formal curriculum about citizenship and community involvement are weak. Brooks' research showed that of 21 students who had been involved in voluntary activity, only a small minority could recall any occasions where they had discussed political or social issues or had talked about community involvement within the context of the formal curriculum. In addition to this, after experience of community involvement, like Mumba, the students reported significant impacts on their political literacy, their confidence in interacting with others and their sense of social and moral responsibility (Brooks, 2005).

Perhaps universities need to rethink their role in promoting connections between formal constructions of knowledge and disciplines and informal learning, facilitating student engagement in the community and thus providing broader, more fluid constructions of academic disciplines.

The global citizen and multi-literacy

Beyond university, graduates will be required to function in complex contemporary environments and respond to the demands of a culturally and linguistically diverse globalised society. Much recent literature and research in this field has suggested that the professional, personal and learning contexts that students are currently in and are aiming for are changed. Business, design and engineering industries are global in nature, and staff may work in distributed teams with colleagues from across the world. People are more mobile for work and in their personal lives, and are in immediate contact with social networks all over the world. These new global contexts require different sorts of literacies, a wider portfolio of literacies, that range from the ability to work with a wide range of sources, media and images to intercultural understandings and an ability to adapt linguistically and socially. These changed environments span personal and professional lives.

John Paul's account talks of the development of multi-literacy through an interweaving of community and university learning. He has developed a huge variety of skills, competences in languages, organisational and personal skills drawn from social interaction and the crossing of educational and social cultures within one country's context. His personal and academic experience as a whole have enabled him to develop a wide range of different competences and the ability to operate in complex social networks. John Paul's account of his learning experiences shows that the combination of his university and community learning has enabled him to secure high-quality employment. Future models of university learning should perhaps reflect unpredictable and changing career paths where you need to know about more that one field (Fearn, 2010). However, John Paul's account also emphasises that whilst his involvement in community has developed his employability, his work has an ethical and civic element that derives from his wish to support others experiencing what he has experienced himself. John Paul's version of citizenship is not synonymous with employability, but involves developing multiple perspectives that enable him as a graduate to understand multiple value systems.

The global citizen and boundary crossings

The crossing of the boundaries between the university and the community may be a way forward in making university learning meaningful and enabling students to develop as responsible, ethical and globally aware citizens. As Kress (2000) suggests, this may require a shift in the locus of control of learning, a dissolution of the frame around the university and community, and 'a change in relation between institution and community, from making the community `come to you', to going out to the community' (Kress, 2000, p. 136). It is important to note that meanings are grounded in real-world patterns of experience, action and subjective interest. This is what the New London Group describe as the 'pedagogical 'weavings'… between school learning and the practical out-of-school experiences of learners.' They note that these kinds of cross-connections between education and the rest of life are 'cultural weavings' (Cope & Kalantzis, 2009). Thus in future university curricula there may be a need for knowledge to be 'contextualised, applied, transdisciplinary and not necessarily carried out in universities' (Manathunga, 2009, p. 131).

Claire's account of her crossing between the contexts of university and community (and back again) brings into the university marginalised voices, including subaltern knowledge. Her interest in public poetry as part of her literature degree motivated her to become involved in promoting access to literature for disempowered groups. She extended her discipline knowledge into the community, blurring the sometimes inflexible boundaries between community and curriculum. Her learning in the community public poetry project fed back into the development of her dissertation, although she acknowledges that the privilege represented in the public poetry role of the poet laureate in her dissertation was in sharp contrast to the community creative writing (whose literary value was no less, she emphasises). A different perspective on literature is brought into the university through Claire applying her alternative, community understanding of public poetry to the establishment view of the poet laureate.

To term the sort of work that Mumba, John Paul and Claire engaged in as 'extra-curricular' is an outdated view of university learning. It implies that the only important knowledge or learning occurs inside the classroom within the confines of the formal curriculum. A university education for the future needs to see the formal and informal curriculum as interconnected. Addressing global perspectives in university learning should not be viewed as an 'add-on', however, and representation and reflection of informal learning within the curriculum is crucial. Subedi notes: 'Add-on frameworks do not consistently or ethically integrate marginalised global knowledge into curriculum' (2010, p. 3).

Concluding Remarks

The student data presented in this paper has underlined the importance of broader educational experiences, emerging from and linked to students' disciplines. Learning in the formal curriculum is of crucial importance, but it is students' interpretation and wider application of that curriculum in communities and social networks that will engage them with their disciplines beyond university. Understanding the lived learning experience of students and seeing what students are doing with their curricula beyond university, how they are taking it and using it in their lives and experience, should tell us something about how we should be shaping university learning for the future.

If global perspectives are to be incorporated into university learning, there may be a need to think about this in a different way. It is suggested in this chapter that to include a critical global perspective in higher education it may be necessary to question what we understand as knowledge and learning, recognising 'subaltern knowledge' and incorporating 'the kinds of knowledge that has been viewed as unworthy to be learned in schools' (Subedi, 2010, p. 3). We may also need to recognise that 'our knowledge is imperfect, provisional, subject to revision in the face of new evidence' (ibid). As a result of this, future university learning may need to be quite different: less rigid, less formal and less confined within disciplines.

References

Beard, C., Clegg, S. & Smith, K. (2007). Acknowledging the affective in Higher Education. *British Educational Research Journal 33*(2), 235–252.

Bourn, D., McKenzie, A. & Shiel, C. (2006). *The Global University: The Role of the Curriculum*. London: Development Education Association.

Brooks, R. (2005). The impact of extra-curricular activities on young people's understandings of citizenship. *British Educational Research Association Research Intelligence, 93*, 8–11.

Cope, B. & Kalantzis, M. (2000). *Multiliteracies: literacy, learning and the design of social futures*. New York: Routledge.

Cope, B. & Kalantzis, M. (2009). "Multiliteracies": New Literacies, New Learning. *Pedagogies: An International Journal, 4*(3), 164–195. Retrieved July 9, 2010 from **http://newlearningonline.com/~newlearn/wp-content/uploads/2009/03/m-litspaper13apr08.pdf**

Denzin, N.K. & Lincoln, Y.S. (2003). *Collecting and interpreting qualitative materials*. California: Sage.

Fearn,. H (2010, February 4). Extreme Makeover. *Times Higher Educational Supplement*, 38–41.

Gullikers, J. (2004, June). *Perceptions of authentic assessment*. Paper presented at the second biannual joint Northumbria/EARLI SIG assessment conference, Bergen.

Haigh, M. (2008). Internationalisation, planetary citizenship and Higher Education Inc. *Compare: a Journal of Comparative and International Education, 38*(4), 427–440.

Kalantzis, M. & Cope, B. (2005). *Learning by Design*. Melbourne Australia: VSIC, Common Ground.

Kalantzis, M. & Cope, B. (2010). Foreword. In D.L. Pullen & D.R. Cole, *Multiliteracies and Technology Enhanced Education: Social Practice and the Global Classroom* (xiii–xv). Hershey, USA: Information Science Reference.

Kress, G. (2000). A Curriculum for the Future. *Cambridge Journal of Education, 30*(1), 133–145.

Manathunga, C. (2009). Post-colonial perspectives on interdisciplinary researcher identities. In A. Brew & L. Lucas (Eds.) *Academic Research and Researchers* (pp. 131–145). Maidenhead McGraw Hill: Open University Press.

Montgomery, C. (2009). A Decade of Internationalisation: has it influenced students' views of cross-cultural group work at university? *Journal of Studies in International Education, 13*(2) 256–270.

Razbully, S. & Bamber, P. (2008, July). *Cross Curricula Planning and the Global Dimension at Liverpool Hope.* Seminar given at Education for Sustainable Development and Global Citizenship ITE Network Inaugural Conference.

Rennie, J. (2010). Rethinking Literacy in Culturally Diverse Classrooms. In D. L. Pullen & D.R. Cole, *Multiliteracies and Technology Enhanced Education: Social Practice and the Global Classroom* (pp. 83–99). Hershey, USA: Information Science Reference.

Shultz, L. & Jorgenson, S. (2010). *Global Citizenship Education in Post-Secondary Institutions: A Review of the Literature.* Retrieved July 9, 2010 from **http://www.uofaweb.ualberta.ca/uai_globaleducation/pdfs/ GCE_lit_review.pdf**

Subedi, B. (2010). *Critical Global Perspectives: Rethinking Knowledge about Global Societies.* USA: Information Age Publishing.

The New London Group (1996). A Pedagogy of Multiliteracies: Designing Social Futures. *Harvard Educational Review. 66*(1), Spring, 1–27.

Trahar, S. (2011). *Developing cultural capability in international higher education: a narrative enquiry.* Oxford: Routledge.

White, C. & Openshaw, R. (2005). *Democracy at the crossroads: International perspectives on critical global citizenship education.* New York: Lexington Books.

The challenge of global citizenship education in the 21st century university: A case for service-learning and community volunteering ?

11

Vivienne Caruana

Abstract

This chapter discusses how universities and their students are influenced by globalisation processes and discourse, the demands of knowledge economies, and notions of cosmopolitanism in conceptualising global citizenship education. It is argued that whilst the principles of participation and responsibility inform notions of global citizenship education in higher education (HE) contexts, activism remains an issue. It is also contended that curriculum and pedagogy that enables engagement with 'self' and 'otherness' without engaging with issues may produce graduates as cosmopolitans rather than graduates as global citizens, a process which requires opportunities to develop qualities and insights that transcend narrow visions of learning in HE to address civic as well as economic and loosely defined moral aspirations. The chapter goes on to suggest that service-learning and community volunteering offer distinct possibilities in delivering the curriculum and pedagogy to provide for global citizenship education in higher education that reflects the fundamental principles of participation, responsibility and activism.

Globalisation and knowledge economies: the context of 'graduates as global citizens'

Globalisation is popularly characterised by increased velocity and density of information flows, the speeding up of time, the collapse of time and the breaking down of national barriers, with technological advances representing both cause and effect. On a personal level, communication and information networks, mass media culture and global community culture increasingly invade our private spaces to propagate a 'market-place' philosophy that tends towards homogeneity, thereby masking the diversity which exists particularly among adolescents. At best media images encourage unreflexive engagement with diversity influencing consumption patterns. Thus engagement with diversity simply determines tastes in food, dress, or music. whilst promoting indulgence in heavily packaged or mediated cultural and tourist experiences (Marshall, 2009; Gunesch, 2004; Skrbis et al, 2004; Blackmore, 2002; The New London Group, 1996). Popular media discourses to which young people are exposed compound this superficial engagement with diversity based on consumption since they tend towards either '...radical ideological indoctrination or forms of oppositional discourse...' that at best '...reinforce existing bias or at worst, are outlandish and irresponsible...' (Cornwell & Stoddard, 2006, p. 26).

In wider social contexts the rapid flow of images, people and goods creates global interdependencies where local events are shaped by global phenomena, blurring the boundaries between home and away, local and global, here and there. These international flows are, of course, not new but what is new is the compression of the world so the awareness of the world as an entity is heightened. Whilst globalisation is undoubtedly about real processes (social, economic and political), these are generated in unequal, divergent and sometimes contradictory ways. In a world of the 'globalisers' and the 'globalised', globalisation is also discourse perpetuated by those who benefit from it. As a liberal ideological construct giving primacy to economic relations it has, in the past, been associated with national or local discourses concerning privatisation, marketisation, managerialisation and commodification (Shultz & Shelane, 2008; Rizvi, 2007; Schattle, 2007; Gacel-Avila, 2005; Naidoo & Jamieson, 2005; Skrbis et al, 2004; Norris, 2003; Blackmore, 2002).

Knowledge economies are both a driving force and outcome of globalisation underpinned by technological advances. As information and communication technology has spewed out more and more information, so it has become a principal source of national economic wealth, and universities have come to play a pivotal role in knowledge production, transfer and dissemination in pursuit of economic prosperity (Blackmore, 2002). Paradoxically, whilst global information is expanding faster than we can comprehend it, a pragmatic-technicist view of work prevails where productivity derives from instrumentalist forms of knowing within a team-orientated labour process (Mocombe, 2004). According to The New London Group (1996) the world of 'post-Fordism' and 'fast capitalism' is based on flattened hierarchies in the workplace, where the qualities of commitment, responsibility and motivation are developed through a workplace culture which weds members of an organisation to corporate vision, mission and values. Within organisational structures, vertical chains of command and control are replaced by horizontal relationships based on a kind of workplace pedagogy. The 'Fordist' division of labour into minute deskilled components is replaced by the 'multi-skilled' workforce sufficiently flexible and adaptable to conduct complex and integrated work in an ever-changing environment. As technical and systems thinkers these workers will have learned how to learn, they will have the ability to think and speak for themselves, will be capable of critique and will be empowered, innovative and creative (Mocombe, 2004; The New London Group, 1996).

In response to the labour demands of knowledge economies, universities are obliged to provide students with the opportunity to develop the skills for access to new forms of work through learning the new language of work; but the central concern of this chapter is whether this is sufficient to prepare graduates capable of dealing with the 'super-complexity' (Barnett, 2000) which will be a phenomenon of their everyday lives as global citizens. A university curriculum and pedagogy which focuses primarily on knowledge economy skills suggests a learning environment where teachers assume the role of technocrats producing docile, compliant workers, thereby compounding what has been termed the 'ignorance explosion' (Lukasiewicz, 1994 as cited in Barnett, 2000) where academic texts become information to be handled, rather than understood, interpreted and adjudicated within the context of a world characterised by uncertainty, challengeability and unpredictability (Barnett, 2002; The New London Group, 1996). It is argued here that in shaping universities' responses to the labour demands of the knowledge economy and validating the claims they can legitimately make in terms of producing graduates as global citizens, perceptions of global citizenship education particularly within the context of an internationalised curriculum will be a key determining factor.

Conceptualising Global Citizenship Education in Higher Education – the Challenges

The internationalised curriculum: global citizenship or cosmopolitanism?

The key principles of citizenship are generally regarded as participation, responsibility and activism. The literature suggests the possibility of university graduates becoming global reformers, global managers, global cosmopolitans, elite global business people or capitalists. They may become trans-national activists or join the ranks of the earth-literate. Particular citizenship roles are thus implied by the variety of academic disciplines on offer in universities. However, in a broader context citizenship scholars fundamentally disagree on the development of international society and the nature of global citizenry, some claiming that national citizenship is giving way to trans-national citizenship whilst others claim that national citizenship is resilient (Shultz & Shelane, 2008; Lagos 2002: Schuster & Solomos, 2002; Falk, 1993;).

The controversies surrounding global versus national identity will in themselves influence the value placed upon global citizenship education in university settings. Furthermore, Isin and Turner (2007) argue that the cosmopolitanism revolving around the changes to mobility and transactions arising from globalisation processes, is a more accurate characterisation of the evolution of 'citizenship' structures in an international context. Cosmopolitanism may be defined as 'feeling at home in the world', straddling the local and the global, having an interest in diversity – looking, listening, intuiting, reflecting – and perhaps becoming the connoisseur of some cultures whilst a dilettante in the majority of them (Gunesch, 2004). Much of the discourse of the 'internationalised curriculum' is a discourse of cosmopolitanism under the influence of globalised business structures which encourage the development of a market for internationally-oriented and qualified graduates. This discourse has in recent years been modified with the emergence of the concept of 'Internationalisation at Home' (Shiel, 2006 as cited in Brookes & Becket, 2010; Caruana & Spurling, 2007).

The emergence of 'Internationalisation at Home' has meant that nowadays, universities are increasingly aware of the need to produce graduates who are capable of working in a society where cross-cultural capability is essential to their employment, whether that be overseas or in their local community. Thus it may be argued, connectivity between the global and the local dimensions in terms of experience and interaction becomes the cornerstone of informed, ethical and responsible decision-making processes based on partnership and social entrepreneurship (Shiel, 2006; Stevens & Campbell, 2006, both cited in Brookes & Becket, 2010). Nonetheless, the emphasis remains more on global perspectives and global competencies rather than global citizenship in any civic sense.

Cosmopolitanism is likely to be influential in shaping not only notions of the internationalised curriculum, but also the role of universities in providing global citizenship education. After all, international academic mobility has been an essential characteristic of universities over centuries of development, pre-dating any process which might be labelled globalisation (Caruana & Spurling, 2007). Furthermore, if global citizenry is indeed something of a myth in the international society of the 21st century, as argued by citizenship scholars like Isin and Turner (2007), legitimisation of universities' involvement in supporting global citizenship education is likely to require recourse back to the social, economic, political and cultural constraints and pressures experienced within globalised higher education settings, just as internationalisation is regarded as the response to globalisation influences.

Universities' responses to globalisation in shaping Global Citizenship Education

In responding to the forces of globalisation the literature suggests three broad possibilities – a neo-liberal approach, a transformationalist approach and a more radical alternative. A neo-liberal approach to globalisation engenders a predominant emphasis on global economic participation rather than responsibility and activism. In this scenario enhancing the ability of individuals (perhaps in already privileged positions) to travel assumes a priority. Particularly in the context of 'widening participation' universities might also seek to extend the boundaries of, and reduce the barriers to, such participation through interventions which encourage open-mindedness and an awareness of the different lands, peoples and ways of life which contribute towards global diversity. This 'human capital' approach to global citizenship education emphasises the need to accumulate a new form of cultural capital in a highly competitive, globalised world of knowledge economies. The business elite are rich in cultural, intellectual and social capital (concepts, connections and competence), and universities may simply be reproducing the citizen of the advanced liberal-democratic 'national' state, the privileged individual who just so happens to be mobile (Shultz & Shelane, 2008; Skrbis et al, 2004). Scorza (2004) argues that most disciplines favour this kind of market model of global citizenship education, preparing graduates for success in a global marketplace '...touting the professional benefits of their offerings in the face of global competition...' This position is understandable since in a globalised world universities must compete for student enrolments. However, as globalisation encourages the professionalisation of universities in order to maintain the competitive edge, some have argued that rather than producing 'graduates as global citizens', universities have contributed towards a decline of civic engagement and a fundamental crisis of public confidence in social and political institutions (London, 1999).

A transformationalist approach to globalisation suggests an alternative model of global citizenship education which is rooted in the mutual interdependence arising from globalisation which strengthens cosmopolitanism as a 'progressive, humanistic ideal' based on universalism, intolerance of human suffering and commitment to protect diversity (Calcutt et al, 2009; Beck & Szneider, 2006; Gunesch, 2004). Thus the emphasis on global perspectives and global competencies to foster participation is complemented by a sense of responsibility, particularly within the context of the local/global interface. Responsibility involves a commitment to openness which seeks to include and engage others within a complex set of local, national and international relationships. Whilst this approach is more akin to a model of global citizenship education which addresses the three key principles of participation, responsibility and activism, it remains problematic; particularly in the sense of how one interprets openness.

Openness is a key concept underpinning both the human capital approach and the moral transformationalist approach to global citizenship education. However, authors have challenged the meaning of openness as a vague concept which particularly in global contexts is diffuse and ill-defined in terms of observable practices. A key issue for example, is whether openness is consciously assumed or circumstantially induced. In this context notions of openness and global connectedness have been characterised as 'banal' and '...taken for granted amongst the public as they are in the media...' (Szerszynski, Urry & Myers in Smith, 2000, 107) Furthermore, it has been argued that the individual 'intoxicated' by 'unspecified openness' and universalism is a 'risky fantasy', in that perceived detachment from the nation state may give rise to no compunction to pay taxes (Skrbis et al, 2004). Openness particularly in the context of the 'global.com' society may be portrayed as '...individuals without commitment, industries without liabilities, news without a public conscience and dissemination of information without a sense of boundaries or discretion...' (Benhabib, 2002:182 as cited in O'Sullivan & Pashby, 2008).

This particular brand of openness, conflated with idealistic sentiment of the moral persuasion which indulges in excessive self-reflexivity, may generate a politically naïve kind of cross-cultural goodwill or what has been termed 'soft' global citizenship education. In this model global citizenship emerges as a politically neutral or banal concept, '...promoting a new civilising mission...' to a generation willing to assume the 'burden' of saving, civilising or educating the world, under the influence of media images and slogans that emphasise the need to be charitable, compassionate and active in acknowledging moral obligation to humanity (Calcutt et al, 2009;

Mendieta, 2008; Andreotti, 2006). Global citizenship education in universities may in fact be reinforcing a sense of individual responsibility without collective consciousness and activism. Berberet (2002, 92) refers to universities' current 'detached objectivity' which is in sharp contrast to the 1960s '...scholarship of protest and relativity...' where '...epistemology [was validated by] community experience...' This detachment is in stark contrast to the radical approach to globalisation and a critical stance on global citizenship education, which would enable students to critically explore global structures that create and perpetuate inequalities, and prepare them to participate in local and national institutions which can provide a counter-weight to the forces of globalisation (Shultz & Shelane, 2008).

Student responses to globalisation in shaping global citizenship education

Clearly notions of global citizenship education are contingent in institutional settings, but they are also contestable from an individual perspective. In an era where the 'student voice' is gaining credibility in shaping university curricula and pedagogy, global citizenship education is also influenced by student dispositions. Scorza (2004) notes in the US context the 'paradoxical gap' between global power and the global competency of citizens, arguing that the more confident young people are in their unequal (but superior) power the less likely they are to feel the need to acquire global competencies equal to, or at least sufficient for, their vast collective power.

This paradox of competency and power rests on two assumptions. Firstly, the less politically informed and capable citizens believe themselves to be, the less civically responsible they feel. Secondly, citizens tend to avoid becoming politically informed and capable because they feel intuitively that this would cause them to incur greater civic responsibility. The paradox is exaggerated within the global context where it is more difficult to stay informed, where there is so much more to know and problems seem beyond comprehension and sometimes out of reach. In effect, '...the scale of global affairs dwarfs the individual...' making it difficult to comprehend one's place in the world and the relationship of that place to global problems. As overwhelming as global issues might appear, it is equally the case that global citizenship in the civic sense may be seen as irrelevant by students, offering them little incentive to engage in the face of diminishing career prospects, corporate downsizing, wage deflation and unprecedented student loan debt. However, some students do actively pursue global engagement – particularly through travel – in a quest for cultural competence which might give them the competitive edge (Andreotti, 2006; Scorza, 2004).

Bourn (2010) provides evidence which suggests a high degree of scepticism around the term 'global citizen' among students, some going so far as to regard it as an elitist concept. However, he also challenges the predominance of stereotypes of students pursuing self-interest over social justice, by going on to argue that through social networking students are in fact, creating a new model of global citizenship using their own forms of dialogue, learning and action. Perhaps in the face of learning opportunities which are exclusively addressing the principles of participation and responsibility, within an overarching framework of globalisation and knowledge economies which perpetuate models of 'soft' global citizenship education, some students are finding other outlets for self-expression and activism extraneous to their 'higher learning' experience. A key question is: how can or should curriculum and pedagogy within university settings connect with and harness this latent activism, in order to produce graduates as global citizens?

Challenging 'Soft' Global Citizenship Education: The possibilities of Service-Learning and Community Volunteering

This chapter thus far has addressed the significance of globalisation and the demands of knowledge economies in shaping how universities and their students conceptualise global citizenship education. Key considerations within the debate have been the influence of the pragmatic-technicist view of the world of work within knowledge economies, and the significance of alternative ideological responses to globalisation within universities. It has been argued that the 'human-capital' and moral approaches to global citizenship education tend to predominate within university settings; approaches which partially address the principles of participation and responsibility but signally neglect the principle of activism.

A major aim of higher education must be to prepare students for the labour market, as suggested by the human-capital approach. It might also be reasonable to assume that promoting respect for humanity's differences and cultural wealth is a legitimate goal, as implied by the model of 'soft' global citizenship education. However, Gacel-Avila (2005) argues that global consciousness necessitates a sense of political responsibility, which is the prerequisite of activism or real engagement with the forces of globalisation, in the context of local and national institutions. This creates an essential problem for global citizenship education in HE, in that it may be seen to be promoting a political agenda. In effect 'soft' global citizenship education offers an easy alternative where the civilising mission can readily substitute for any sense of political responsibility which addresses the roots of inequalities in a globalised world (Andreotti, 2006).

How to enable activism whilst avoiding any suggestion of political bias is perhaps the real underlying challenge of global citizenship education in HE which requires us, firstly, to explore the ways in which we can provide a learning environment which enables students to develop the knowledge and virtues with which they can understand their experience. Secondly, in a globalised world of 'supercomplexity', curriculum and pedagogy should not only develop student voices – enabling them to speak up, to negotiate and to engage with their own sense of self in order to function in the world of work – but should also provide the space to critically engage with the conditions of their and others' working lives in order to envisage different lifeworlds (Barnett, 2000; Brookes & Becket, 2010; The New London Group, 1996). Simply responding to the labour demands of the knowledge economy is likely to perpetuate a reductionist approach to learning, where it is mistaken for extant knowledge or skills and strategies to be acquired and is thus disembodied from students' lived experience. Cornwell and Stoddard (2006, 30) argue teaching for citizenship is a process of creating a complex and multiple 'truth' or 'reality' which involves contestation and negotiation rather than encouraging students to '...rest content with the self-serving views presented in the mainstream culture...'

A central proposition of this chapter however, is that curriculum and pedagogy that enables engagement with 'self' and 'otherness' may produce graduates as cosmopolitans rather than graduates as global citizens. Global citizenship education requires opportunities to develop qualities and insights that transcend narrow visions of learning in higher education but also address civic as well as economic and loosely defined moral aspirations, thereby embracing the principle of activism without engendering political bias. This in turn requires a focus on developing the skills of public problem solving at the local/global interface, which help people to achieve common ends through the ability to frame issues in public terms whilst engaging with 'otherness' to pursue new courses of action (London, 1999).

Service-learning and community volunteering offer distinct possibilities in delivering the curriculum and pedagogy to provide for global citizenship education in higher education that reflects the fundamental principles of participation, responsibility and activism. However, to date there is relatively little research to evaluate these kinds of interventions in the context of globalisation and global citizenship education in higher education settings. Service-learning in particular has traditionally embraced an action-orientated focus on practice, without addressing theoretical perspectives to provide an underpinning rationale. In some ways this has contributed towards its marginalisation within academia. The Michigan Journal for Community Service-Learning established in 1994 has gone some way towards increasing academic legitimacy, extending teachers' and students' understanding by addressing theory, practice, method and research at least in the US context. An important landmark event is the First International Conference on Service-Learning Research held in 2001. A more significant recent development in 2008–9, acknowledging the expansion of the HE civic engagement movement (at least in the US), is the broadening of the journal's purview to include articles about campus-community partnerships and engaged scholarship. Nonetheless, the journal's contributors and possibly readership remain predominantly North American in origin (National Service-Learning Clearing House website, 2011; IPSL website, 2010; Gills & Eyler, 1994; Chan Cheung Ming & Ma Hok Ka, n.d.; Michigan Journal for Community Service-Learning website, n.d.).

It is significant that both service-learning and community volunteering in universities pre-date the era of globalisation. The phrase service-learning was first coined in 1967 to describe a project that linked the students and faculty of Oak Ridge Associated Universities with tributary development organisations in East Tennessee, USA. It has since (some authors would argue mistakenly) been associated with the 'make-work' schemes of Franklin D. Roosevelt's 'New Deal' in response to the unemployment of the 1930s

Great Depression, and with the post-war US non-military national service schemes and government offers of educational opportunity in return for service to country. In recent years service-learning has been firmly associated with the mission and philosophy of higher education particularly in the US; challenging rationalist views of higher learning as an end in itself, serving 'students as customers' devoid of aspirational goals. Students' voluntary action has a long history particularly in the UK, originating in 'mission' and 'settlement' movements arising out of the religious societies formed at universities during the evangelical revival. Significantly, during the 1960s a focus on social service gave way to 'community action', representing a shift towards a more politicised understanding of voluntary service. In more recent times however, whilst many students continue to be involved in student-led activities they are also likely to pursue volunteering placements through a university unit (National Service-Learning Clearing House website, 2011; IPSL website, 2010; Williams, 2009; Gills & Eyler, 1994; Brewis, n.d.: Students volunteering and social action: histories and policies website, n.d.; Chan Cheung Ming & Ma Hok Ka, n.d.).

The Atlanta Service-Learning conference held in 1969 defines service-learning as '...the integration of the accomplishment of a needed task with educational growth...' the goals of which include '...to add breadth and depth and relevance to students' learning' and 'to give young people, ...front-line experience with today's problems so they will be better equipped to solve them as adult citizens'. (Atlanta Service-Learning Conference Report, 1970, iii). Partnership is a key principle – students learn from the service agency and from the community, whilst directing their efforts to address community needs, which in turn enables the community to learn from students. Thus service learning makes academic study applicable and relevant through practical experience, providing the environment where the theory of academic study is field-tested, enabling students to critically analyse learning in the context of service. At the same time service is informed by academic study through knowledge, analysis and reflection (IPSL website, 2010; Williams, 2009; Gills & Eyler, 1994; McAleavey, n.d.).

Whilst work placement or internship provides opportunities for the application of knowledge, service learning differs fundamentally in the emphasis placed on students exploring with the community how their education may benefit the community and well-being of others. Thus it is argued here that service-learning has potential to transcend pragmatic-technicist approaches to higher learning and both the human-capital and moral approaches to global citizenship education, by developing the skills and dispositions which support inquiry in public contexts in order to envisage alternative courses of action.

The literature on the practice of service-learning does in fact, lay claim to a wide range of benefits all of which may be regarded as critical to global citizenship education, although these have not been adequately tested in higher education environments. Practitioners argue that in relating learning to the outside world, students effectively explore the social context of its usability. They confront complexity, uncertainty and ethical issues head-on, effectively making their knowledge 'actionable' or portable to new situations and circumstances. In effect, a 'humanistic' perspective is at the core of the service-learning experience which involves '...engaging in ...un-learning, re-learning and new learning...' (Goddard & Sinclair, 2008).

As well as providing portable, deeper and long-lasting learning, service-learning practitioners claim heightened intercultural and international understanding, global awareness and socially responsible citizenship as outcomes of the learning experience. Learning tends to take place in collaboration with people whose lives are often very different and hence learners come to appreciate their experiences, ideas and values. A sense of shared identity with others as human beings is juxtaposed with a more acute awareness of one's own complex identity encompassing world views, realities and a set of values that are not necessarily universally shared (Furco, 2010; Goddard & Sinclair, 2008; Ehrlich n.d.; McAleavey, n.d.).

In contrast to service-learning, university volunteering schemes are not tied directly to a particular field of academic or professional study: but similarly to service-learning, they provide immersion in real-world experience which can potentially challenge reductionist views of the world as shaped by formal learning experiences. Volunteering schemes also have a dual orientation, claiming potential benefits for community (not only in terms of immediate physical benefits but also for ongoing partnerships between university and community) and for students. Most schemes highlight the possibility of the development of skills including communication, leadership, teamwork and planning and organisation through volunteering experiences. Personal benefits are also claimed, such as 'making a difference' and 'helping a cause close to your heart' (NUI Galway, 2010).

Universities like Leeds Metropolitan in England and NUI Galway in Ireland, for example, offer a diverse range of local community volunteering opportunities to students. Leeds Metropolitan is particularly well known for its pioneering work in international volunteering (Jones, 2010; Killick, 2007). The international volunteering programme which began in 2007 has supported the involvement of some 650 staff and students in '...affordable, safe, meaningful, challenging and rewarding experiences...' whilst sustaining '...beneficial relationships with [the University's] community partners overseas...' and '...supporting Internationalisation at Leeds Met.' (http://www.leedsmet.ac.uk/cpv/index_About.htm, n.d.)

The programme provides a short-term opportunity (usually two to four weeks) for participants to develop global perspectives through community and conservation projects across six continents. Projects are developed with existing partners, either universities or charitable foundations, already supported through fund-raising initiatives (Jones, 2010).

The University's Community Partnership and Volunteering web-page states 'Our aim is simple: to help more students and staff of Leeds Met to engage in volunteer work both in Leeds and abroad. Why? Because volunteering enhances our personal and professional development and because Leeds Met has a commitment to support its many Community Partners.' (http://www.leedsmet.ac.uk/cpv/, n.d.) The volunteering web-pages state '...a strong commitment to enhancing the employability skills of all our volunteers...'a theme which informs '...the way the programme works: the application and selection process, team sessions on employability and being a reflective practitioner' (http://www.leedsmet.ac.uk/cpv/index_About.htm, n.d.)

Whilst employability considerations mirroring the human-capital approach to global citizenship education are apparent, Jones' (2010, p. 93) research with a small group of Leeds Metropolitan University's international volunteers reveals that a key consideration for volunteers themselves is feeling that they are '...making a difference... ' a disposition which is characteristic of cosmopolitanism of the moral persuasion and 'soft' global citizenship education. Whilst acknowledging that international volunteering programmes might simply provide more opportunities for those '...already engaged...', Jones (2010, p. 95) also claims that volunteers' lives have nonetheless been transformed. They have come to '...doubt the superiority of their own cultural values...' (Jones, 2010, p. 92), an attribute essential in closing the paradoxical gap between global power and global competency of citizens rehearsed earlier in this chapter. In effect, volunteers learn about themselves, about cultural 'others', and about group empathy; and challenge previously held views and stereotypes through processes like putting themselves in other peoples' shoes, being in the minority, sharing humanity, finding connections, considering others' perspectives and reviewing their own cultural assumptions (Jones, 2010, p. 92).

Community volunteering, like service-learning, appears to offer potential in providing education for global citizenship in higher education, although there are issues particularly in relation to the principles of inquiry and reflection. According to Dewey (1933) whilst all education is experience, not all experience is educative. The educative experience involves inquiry not only as a means of becoming informed, but also as a means of communicating interests, creating public opinion and making decisions. In contrast with service-learning the general absence of any structured opportunities to reflect on experience, particularly in the context of academic study, may be significant in determining how engagement with global perspectives through international volunteering relates to the possibilities for future activism. Evidence suggests that international volunteers engage with 'self' and 'other', thereby challenging tendencies towards narrow-mindedness and inward-oriented perspectives; but in the absence of any formal connection to the mainstream curriculum, the degree to which students engage with issues on the ground may be limited. In short, whilst much learning within the formal curriculum in the absence of service-learning represents engagement with issues but not with people or community (particularly other people who view the world through different lenses), community volunteering provides engagement with the people but not with the issues, if it is undertaken as extra-curricular activity.

Conclusions

This chapter has explored conceptions of global citizenship in higher education which, it is concluded, are generally modelled on the principles of either human-capital accumulation through cross-cultural consumption, or 'soft' global citizenship and moral obligation. It is argued that under globalisation and the attendant need to prepare students for the labour market as it exists within knowledge economies, learning in formal university settings may tend towards the mechanistic, instrumentalist, pragmatic and reductionist. The central proposition is that in order to prepare 'graduates as global citizens', pedagogy needs to address real-world contexts enabling students to connect their experience and their learning to that world and, perhaps more importantly, to challenge familiar and typical practices, norms, values and beliefs encountered in their higher education learning experience.

Community volunteering enables students to view the world through alternative lenses and to challenge self-interest, acknowledge and perhaps even empathise with 'other'. Service-learning as an integrated component of curriculum, exploring the relationship between community and 'conscious educational growth', may go further in enhancing social and political awareness through a process of inquiry and reflection to '...de-naturalize and make strange what they have learned...re-framing knowledge within wider discourses...gaining personal and theoretical distance...' (The New London Group, 1996, p. 21). In this way graduates may become the global citizens who are not only globally competent and informed, but also willing to engage contestation and negotiation in the quest for alternative ways of knowing, doing, being and becoming.

This paper therefore calls for educational research into service-learning and community volunteering which re-visits and re-assesses priorities in a globalised world, evaluates practice, and perhaps re-affirms the importance of these relatively marginal and action-orientated learning models in the specific context of global citizenship education in higher education settings. To paraphrase James E. Allen, the US Commissioner of Education, in his address to the inaugural meeting of the ASLC on 30 June, 1969 'Today's youth [in aspiring to become global citizens] want an education geared to realities more vital than theory or things. It is less interested in ideas than values. Young people want their education to take them past knowledge to wisdom and past wisdom to action – the kind of action that can translate their energy and their vision into new patterns of life... This is the positive side of activism.'

References

Andreotti, V. (2006). Soft versus Critical Global Citizenship Education. Open Space for Dialogue and Enquiry. Retrieved January 20, 2011, from

http://www.osdemethodology.org.uk/texts/softcriticalvan.pdf

Allen, J.E. (1969, June). *Educational Needs of Young People Today, Address to the Inaugural Meeting of the Atlanta Service-Learning Conference (ASLC)*. In ASLC (1970) Atlanta Service-Learning Conference Report, Georgia: ASLC.

Atlanta Service-Learning Conference (1970). *Atlanta Service-Learning Conference Report*, Georgia: ASLC .

Barnett, R. (2000). *Realising the University in an Age of Supercomplexity* Buckingham: Society for Research into Higher Education and Open University Press.

Beck, U. & Szneider, N. (2006). Unpacking Cosmopolitanism for the Social Sciences: A Research Agenda. *The British Journal of Sociology, 57*(1), 1–23.

Benhabib, S. (2002). *The claims of culture*. Princeton, N.J.: Princeton University Press.

Berberet, J. (2002). Nurturing an Ethos of Community Engagement. *New Directions for Teaching and Learning Summer 90,* 91–100.

Blackmore, J. (2002). Globalisation and the Restructuring of Higher Education for New Knowledge Economies: New Dangers or Old Habits Troubling Gender Equity Work in Universities. *Higher Education Quarterly, 56*(4), 419–444.

Bourn, D. (2010). Students as Global Citizens. In E. Jones (Ed.) *Internationalisation and the Student Voice: Higher Education Perspectives* (pp. 18–29). Abingdon: Routledge.

Brewis, G. (n.d.) *Students, volunteering and social action: Histories and Policies, Timeline* Retrieved January 30, 2011 from **http://www.studentvolunteeringhistory.org/timeline.html**

Brookes, M & Becket, N. (2010). Developing Global Perspectives Through International Management Degrees. *Journal of Studies in International Education.* Published online Jan 7, 2010. Retrieved June 17, 2011 from **http://jsi.sagepub.com/content/early/2010/01/08/1028315309357 944.abstract**

Calcutt, L., Woodward, I. & Zlatko, S. (2009). Conceptualising Otherness: An Exploration of the Cosmopolitan. *Journal of Sociology, 45*(2), 169–186.

Caruana, V. & Spurling, N. (2007). *The internationalisation of UK higher education: a review of selected material.* York, UK: Higher Education Academy. Retrieved, January 20, 2011 from **http://www.heacademy.ac.uk/assets/York/documents/ourwork/tla/i nternationalisation/lit_review_internationalisation_of_uk_he_v2.pdf**

Chan Cheung Ming, A. & Ma Hok Ka, C. (n.d.) *Service-Learning Theory Development.* Retrieved January 20, 2011, from **http://www.ln.edu.hk /osl/SLRS/Service-Learning%20Theory%20Development.ppt**

Cornwell, G.H. & Stoddard E.W. (2006). Freedom, Diversity and Global Citizenship *Liberal Education 92*(2) Spring, 26–33.

Dewey, J. (1933). *How we Think. A restatement of the relation of reflective thinking to the educative process.* Boston: D.C.Heath

Ehrlich, T (n.d.). *Service-Learning in Undergraduate Education: Where is it going.* Retrieved January 22, 2011 from **http://www.carnegiefoundation.org/perspectives/service-learning-undergraduate-education-where-it-going**

Falk, R. (1993). The Making of Global Citizenship. In J. Brecher, J. Brown Childs & J. Cutler (Eds.). *Global visions: beyond the new world order.* Boston: South End Press.

Furco, A. (2010, January). *Strengthening University-Community Engagement through Service-Learning* Paper presented to Carnegie Research Institute, Leeds Metropolitan University, Leeds, UK.

Gacel-Ávila, J. (2005). The Internationalisation of Higher Education: A Paradigm for Global Citizenry. *Journal of Studies in International Education, 9*(2), 121–136.

Gills, D.E. Jr. & Eyler, J. (1994). The Theoretical Roots of Service-Learning in John Dewey: Towards a Theory of Service-Learning. *Michigan Journal of Community Service-Learning 1*(1), 77–85.

Goddard, T. & Sinclair, K. (2008, January). Transforming professional education: The lost art of service and global citizenship. In *Preparing for the graduate of 2015*. Retrieved January 22, 2011 from **http://otl.curtin.edu.au/tlf/tlf2008/refereed/goddard.html**

Gunesch, K. (2004). Education for Cosmopolitanism: Cosmopolitanism as a Personal Cultural Identity Model for and within International Education. *Journal of Research in International Education. 3*(3): 251–275.

International Partnership for Service-Learning and Leadership (IPSL) (n.d.). Retrieved February 23, 2011 from **http://www.ipsl.org/about/mission**

Isin, E.F. & Turner, B.S. (2007). Investigating citizenship: An agenda for citizenship studies *Citizenship Studies 11*(1): 5–17.

Jones, E. (2010). 'Don't Worry About the Worries' Transforming Lives Through International Volunteering. In E. Jones (Ed.) *Internationalisation and the Student Voice, Higher Education Perspectives* (pp. 83–97.) New York: Routledge.

Killick, D. (2007). Internationalisation and engagement with the wider community. In E. Jones & S. Brown (Eds.), *Internationationalising higher education* (pp. 135–153). Abingdon: Routledge.

Lagos, T.G. (2002). *Global Citizenship – Towards a Definition*. Retrieved January 22, 2011 from: **http://depts.washington.edu/gcp/pdf/globalcitizenship.pdf**

London, S. (1999). The Academy and Public Life: Healing the Rift. *Higher Education Exchange* (Summer), 4–15.

Lukasiewicz, J. (1994). *The Ignorance Explosion, Understanding Industrial Civilisation*. Ontario: Carleton University Press.

Marshall, H. (2009). Educating the European Citizen in the Global Age: Engaging with the Post-national and Identifying a Research Agenda. *Journal of Curriculum Studies, 41*(2), 247–267.

McAleavey, S.J. (n.d.). *Service-Learning: Theory and Rational.* Retrieved January 21, 2011, from **http://www.mesacc.edu/other/ engagement/pathways/rationale.shtml**

Mendieta, E. (2008, December). *From the Abolition of Politics to a Politics of Liberation: Globalizations from Below and the Cosmopolitanism of the Other: A Discussion.* Paper presented at the American Philosophical Association's Easter Division Meeting, Philadelphia, USA. Retrieved January 23, 2011, from **http://www.sju.edu/~jgodfrey/MendietaCosmopolitanism.pdf**

Michigan Journal of Community Service-Learning website (n.d.). Retrieved February 23, 2011, from **http://www.umich.edu/~mjcsl/index.html**

Mocombe, P.C. (2004). *Where Did Freire Go Wrong? Pedagogy in Globalization: The Grenadian Example.* Retrieved February 2, 2011, from **http://www.net4dem.org/mayglobal/Events/Conference%202004/ papers/PaulMocombe.pdf**

Naidoo, R. & Jamieson, I. (2005). Empowering Participants or Corroding Learning? Towards a Research Agenda on the Impact of Student Consumerism in Higher Education. *Journal of Education Policy, 20*(3), 267–281.

National Service Learning Clearing House (n.d.). Retrieved February 2, 2011 from **http://www.servicelearning.org**

The New London Group (1996). A Pedagogy of Multiliteracies: Designing Social Futures. *Harvard Educational Review, 66*(1), 60–92.

Norris, P (2003). Global Governance and Cosmopolitan Citizens. In D. Held & A. McGrew (Eds.) *The Global Transformations Reader: An Introduction to the Globalization Debate* (pp. 287–298). Malden, Mass: Polity Press.

NUI Galway (n.d.). *Thinking of Volunteering, A Step-by-Step guide to Volunteering for NUI Galway Students.* Retrieved February 4, 2011, from **www.nuigalway.ie/alive**

O'Sullivan, M. & Pashby, K.(2008). *Citizenship Education in the Era of Globalization* Rotterdam: Sense Publishers.

Rizvi, F. (2007). Postcolonialism and Globalization in Education. *Cultural Studies, 7*(3), 256–263.

Schattle, H. (2007). *The Practices of Global Citizenship*. Lanham, Maryland: Rowman and Littlefield.

Schuster, L & Solomos, J. (2002). Rights and Wrongs across European Borders: Migrants, Minorities and Citizenship. *Citizenship Studies 6*(1), 37–54.

Shiel, C. (2006) Developing the global citizen, *Academy Exchange*, 5, 18–20.

Shultz, L. & Shelane, J. (2008). *Global Citizenship Education in Post-Secondary Institutions: A Review of the Literature*. Retrieved February 4, 2011, from **http://www.uofaweb.ualberta.ca/ uai_globaleducation/pdfs/GCE_lit_review.pdf**

Skrbis, Z., Kendall, G. & Woodward, I. (2004). Locating Cosmopolitanism. Between Humanist Ideal and Grounded Social Category. *Theory, Culture & Society, 21*(6), 115–136.

Scorza, J.A. (2004, September). *Teaching Global Citizenship: The Paradox of Competency and Power*. Paper presented to the 2004 Annual Meeting of the American Political Science Association, Chicago, Ill.

Stevens, C. & Campbell, P. (2006). Collaborating to connect to global citizenship, information, literacy and lifelong learning in the global studies classroom, *Reference Science Review 34*, 536–556.

Szerszynski, B., Urry, J. & Myers, G. (2000) Mediating Global Citizenship. In J. Smith (Ed.), *The daily globe: environmental change, the public and the media*. London: Earthscan.

Williams, J.W. (2009, February) *Service Learning: Practical Guidance from Theory*. Paper presented at the American Political Science Association Teaching and Learning Conference, Baltimore, Maryland.

Moving on

12

Valerie Clifford and Catherine Montgomery

We hope that this book has engaged you in the debate about the purpose of higher education in the world today. We see our universities as having a responsibility to educate global citizens who are not only highly capable people in their professional spheres but who also recognise their responsibilities as global citizens to act in ways that benefit people locally and globally, not advantaging themselves to the detriment of others.

The contributors to this book have expressed the complexities of globalisation: the rapidity of change, the ambiguity and uncertainty of Barnett's 'supercomplexity' (2000). They have also explored the diversity of responses from higher education institutions, from the 'symbolic' to the 'transformative', from what an institution 'does' to what it 'is' (Turner & Robson, 2008), from the neo-liberal, competitive activities to anti-capitalist, egalitarian, sustainability visions. What all appear to agree is that higher education institutions need to reassess the totality of their students' tertiary education experience and to rebuild their formal and informal curricula for a new future that foregrounds personal integrity and ethics. While many universities have progressed along the Internationalisation of the Curriculum (IoC) path sufficiently to produce 'cosmopolitans', graduates who have some awareness of self and of otherness, they mostly fail to engage students personally with global issues. A greater commitment is required to ensure an education leading to socially responsible, active global citizenship.

The concept of an education for global citizenship, and for leadership, gives the IoC agenda a very strong focus on the difficult areas of personal ethical development. We have begun to explore what this might involve for all our students and for ourselves as teachers. Naturally, it is clear that staff will need to become knowledgeable and involved in this agenda before it can begin to percolate through the curriculum; and here, there is much educational development work to be accomplished. Meanwhile, this book presents some deep reflections from staff and students as they engage actively with otherness, their own self development and curriculum development in their fields. Academics have spent many years augmenting and internalising their knowledge of their disciplines, including the research methodologies, pedagogies and even languages of discourse. For such academic specialists, the challenge of moving into a new, interdisciplinary space of critique and change can be very daunting (Clifford, 2009; Becher & Trowler, 2001; Becher; 1998; Mestenhauser & Ellingboe,1998). Giroux (1992, p. 15) had a vision of teachers assuming new roles as 'transformative intellectuals' who challenge both themselves and their students to cross the self-imposed barriers on the borders of disciplines and cultures, an idea so well illustrated by Holliday in this volume. Giroux (1992) argued that universities need to invite, and support, academics and students to become 'border crossers', to engage in a exploration of their own history and place to reach some understanding of self and of their own culture in relation to others in the global environment. For some, these border crossings will happen at the local level where indigenous knowledges should be celebrated rather than marginalised and inferiorised (Reagan, 2005; Okolie, 2003; Boufoy-Bastick, 2003; Teasdale & Ma Rhea, 2000; Dei, 2000). Gough (1999) envisions these borderlands as transnational spaces where the criss-crossing of new and increasingly complex patterns of interconnectedness destabilise relationships and our own sense of identity. To fuel creative explorations across these ideological borders, by staff and students, we need to create safe spaces for this high-risk work, and support for experimentation with new curricula, new pedagogical relationships, and a re-examination of our own acceptance of the world as given.

As well as our personal commitment and work, it is also clear that IoC requires a whole institution approach. The commitment to develop global citizens, see the learning experiences of students in holistic terms, on and off campus, within both the formal and informal curriculum, requires a vision at the institutional level, and both commitment and resourcing for staff development that is energetically promoted from the highest levels of management. A willingness to research into, and also evaluate honestly, our own practice is one way ahead. We need to encourage our institutions to value and support pedagogical research and to recognise it as an essential part of the change process. It is also imperative to find ways to develop relationships and work with our international colleagues, at home and overseas, that will lead to the sharing of knowledge and experience and to the development of new pedagogical approaches and innovative curricula (Clifford & Henderson, 2011; Clifford et al., 2010). Especially, we need to welcome opportunities to see ourselves and our ideas through non-Western eyes and to learn non-Western perspectives.

In these pages we present a radical, transformative, interpretation of an internationalised curriculum that aims to provide an education for future socially responsible, active global citizens. We have considered the implications at the institutional level of educational objectives and policies, along with the leadership roles of senior and middle management, and have chosen to privilege the research aspects of authors' accounts of their practice. Our journey is ongoing and we believe that research is a stepping stone to the next phase of IoC, the evaluation of global citizenship education. We now need to engage with the complex area of evaluation, to stimulate more attention to holistic curriculum development for internationalisation; and to demonstrate to universities and to students, not only the effectiveness of the work being undertaken, but also the imperative to engage with internationalising the curriculum.

References

Barnett, R. (2000). *Realising the University in an Age of Supercomplexity* Buckingham: Society for Research into Higher Education & Open University Press.

Becher, T. (1989). *Academic tribes and territories: intellectual enquiry and the cultures of the disciplines.* Milton Keynes: Society for Research into Higher Education & Open University Press.

Becher, T. & Trowler, P.R. (2001). *Academic tribes and territories: intellectual enquiry and the cultures of the disciplines.* (Second edition). Buckingham: Open University Press and Society for Research into Higher Education.

Boufoy-Bastick, B. (2003). *Academic attainment and cultural values.* Muenchen: Lincom Europa

Clifford, V. & Henderson, J. (2011, July). Shifting identities: international staff negotiating new academic identities. Paper presented at Higher Education on the Edge HERDSA Conference, Brisbane.

Clifford, V.A. (2009). Engaging the disciplines in internationalising the curriculum. *International Journal of Academic Development, 14*(2),133–143.

Clifford, V. Adetunji, H., Haigh, H., Henderson, J., Spiro, J. & Hudson, J. (2010). *Report on BSLES Project: Fostering Interculturality and Global Perspectives at Brookes through Dialogue with Staff,* Oxford Centre for Staff and Learning Development, Oxford Brookes University, UK.

Dei, G. S. (2000). Rethinking the role of Indigenous knowledges in the academy. *International Journal of Inclusive Education, 4*(2), 111–132.

Giroux, H. (1992). *Border crossings: cultural workers and the politics of education.* New York: Routledge.

Gough, N. (1999). Globalization and school curriculum change: locating a transnational imaginary. *Journal of Education Policy, 14*(1), 73–84.

Mestenhauser, J. & Ellingboe, B. (1998). *Reforming higher education curriculum: Internationalizing the campus.* Phoenix: American Council on Education and Oryx Press.

Okolie, A. C. (2003). Producing knowledge for sustainable development in Africa: implications for higher education. *Higher Education, 46,* 235–260.

Reagan, T. (2005). *Non-western educational traditions. Indigenous approaches to educational thought and practice.* Third edition. New Jersey: Lawrence Erlbaum Associates.

Teasdale, G. R. & Rhea, Z. M. (2000). *Local knowledge and wisdom in higher education.* Oxford: Pergamon.

Turner, Y. & Robson, S. (2008). *Internationalizing the University.* London: Continuum.

Index

International 32-34, 39, 49-51,
57, 80, 124, 164, 170, 177, 180,
213, 216, 217, 232
Mentoring 60, 80

Study abroad 56, 79, 84, 155

Systemic change 73, 84

Sustainability 16, 94, 96, 97, 101,
103, 109, 111, 113, 125,

T
Teaching practices 62

Transformation 30, 40-42, 49, 50,
70, 71, 201, 202, 208, 232-234

U
Universities 14, 15, 18, 19, 21, 27-
42, 49-53, 55, 64, 67-70, 74, 76,
81, 85-89, 93, 94, 98-113, 128,
150, 171, 215, 221, 223, 227, 229,
230-235, 237, 239-243, 253-256

as businesses 37, 50, 110
Australian 16, 47, 50, 51, 54, 55,
57, 70, 73, 74, 76, 79, 81, 87, 91,
93, 110, 104, 110
Indian 93, 99, 108, 113, 173
research-intensive 74, 81, 8
UK 19, 28, 32, 36, 38, 93, 99,
110, 112, 142, 182, 186, 240,
241, 243

V
Value(s) 17, 30, 52, 62, 70, 86, 94,
98, 100, 101, 106, 107, 109, 111,
128, 132, 143, 146, 154, 166, 172,
173, 176-178, 180, 181, 220, 229,
241-246

Volunteering 130, 155, 209, 212,
218, 219, 227, 237, 239, 240-245

W
Western 14, 31, 35, 93, 98, 99,
106, 108, 112, 113, 128-134, 141-
146, 151, 152, 156, 166, 168, 175,
178, 182, 255